Preface

Fifteen years ago I had the privilege of ser‍ a month as a visiting professor at the Institute for Rel‍ nd Human Development, located at the Texas Medical Center in Houston, Texas, in the United States. While there I was asked to deliver a series of public lectures, intended for educated lay people and also doctors, nurses, and staff connected with the center. The topic that I was asked to take as my overall subject was "What it means to be a human person." The lectures were delivered (in March 1974) and were received very kindly by the quite large audiences that came to the center each week to listen to me.

I had no intention of publishing the lectures, but I retained my notes, for what they were worth, with the thought that some of the material might be used on another occasion. As a matter of fact, not one but two occasions arose, within the last two years, when I was able to develop those notes into lectures that (in a slightly altered form) constitute the present small book. The first of the occasions was in 1987, when I was invited by the Reverend Arthur F. McNulty, Jr., rector of Calvary Episcopal Church in Pittsburgh, Pennsylvania, to speak daily for a week at that church. The subject of those talks was the meaning of human existence, in its various relationships, as understood in that sort of theological enquiry with which for many years I have been associated—namely, *Process Theology*.

The second of these occasions was in June 1988. I was invited by the Reverend James W. Evans and his wife,

Margaret Evans, to be the speaker at one of a series of summer meetings they arrange in Wisconsin, where they have been living since retiring from work in Champaign-Urbana, Illinois. These summer sessions, each lasting a week, include music and art, with lectures on some appropriate religious subject. Once again, the topic for my share in the June 1988 session was the meaning of human existence—and again, from the perspective of Process Theology.

Thus, what is here presented is the set of lectures given in Pittsburgh and in Wisconsin, with two chapters added at the beginning. One chapter is an introduction to Christian faith as this is seen by Process Christian thinkers. The other added chapter has to do with the question of evil, in its various forms. The fact of evil in the world and in human experience raises serious questions for *any* Christian discussion, as much about human existence as about the reality and activity of God who in Christian faith is affirmed to be nothing other than "pure unbounded love."

The title given this book, *Becoming and Belonging*, indicates the general approach that I have taken: to exist as human *is* to exist as an instance of "becoming" or developing (for better or worse) and is also to belong with others of our kind in a great enterprise in which each one of us belongs and to which each one of us makes her or his contribution, for good or for ill.

I am grateful to the two places that invited me to give these lectures; I am grateful to the audiences in both places, who listened in a kindly and interested fashion to what I had to say; and above all I am grateful to the McNultys and the Evanses for their hospitality and for their warm friendship, lasting over many years.

Norman Pittenger

King's College
University of Cambridge
England
July 1988

Contents

1

Christian Faith

The title of this book, *Becoming and Belonging*, indicates the two main points that I shall stress in its several chapters. The wider philosophical conceptuality that includes them is that one known today as *Process Thought*, with which I have been working for more than forty years of academic life. That wider conceptuality will be used here for Christian purposes. But the two points that I noted, *becoming* and *belonging*, are especially important for us: the former points to the "processive" or developmental nature of all reality; the latter to the communal or social quality in that reality. My concern is to show that in each of the several topics to be considered—Christianity as an organic whole; the fact of evil known to every one of us; the meaning of human personality in itself, in its familial, and in its social aspects; and the religious community—becoming and belonging must be taken with utmost seriousness.

I write as a Christian—and as a priest of the Anglican church. Hence I believe that human existence is grounded in God who in Christian faith is seen as primal cause and final affect and whose "nature and name," in Charles Wesley's words, is sheer Love. It is one of the tragedies of Christian theology that the divine Love has not always been made central. As Alfred North Whitehead once put it,

> When the religious thought of the ancient world
> from Mesopotamia to Palestine, and from Palestine
> to Egypt, required terms to express that ultimate

1

unity of direction in the universe, upon which all order depends, and which gives meaning to importance, they could find no better way to express themselves than by borrowing the characteristics of the touchy, vain, imperious tyrants who ruled the empires of the world. In the origins of civilised religion, gods are like dictators. Our modern rituals still retain the taint. The most emphatic repudiations of this archaic notion are to be found scattered in the doctrines of Buddhism and in the Christian gospels. (*Modes of Thought,* p. 49)

Whitehead's reference to "the Christian gospels" brings to mind one of his finest utterances, which I shall have occasion to quote again in this chapter. He was speaking of "the supreme moment in religious history, according to Christianity," and he wrote:

The essence of Christianity is the appeal to the life of Christ as a revelation of the nature of God and of his agency in the world. The record is fragmentary, inconsistent, and uncertain. It is not necessary for me to express any opinion as to the proper reconstruction of the most likely tale of historic fact. . . . But there can be no doubt as to what elements in the record have evoked a response from all that is best in human nature. The mother, the Child, and the bare manger: the lowly man, homeless and self-forgetful, with his message of peace, love, and sympathy: the suffering, the agony, the tender words as life ebbed, the final despair: and the whole with the authority of supreme victory. (*Adventure of Ideas,* pp. 170-71)

He then went on to ask, "Can there be any doubt that the power of Christianity lies in its revelation in act, of that which Pilate divined in theory?" (pp. 170-71) By it, he believed "we are delivered from the kinds of theism which would portray God as *the ruling Caesar,* or *the ruthless moralist,* or *the unmoved mover,*" since here the stress is on "the tender elements in the world, which slowly and in

2

quietness operate by love. . . . Love neither rules, nor is it unmoved; also it is a little oblivious as to morals." (*Process and Reality,* pp. 520-21)

I have quoted these passages from Whitehead for two reasons: first, because he is the "founding father" of the Process conceptuality; and second, because what he says in them points to God as "pure unbounded Love" and to our own human existence as intended to be a creaturely love (doubtless imperfect and defective because finite and mortal). Their becoming and their belonging are part of that intended existence. And here is the main theme of this book.

To say this about God requires further discussion. To say it about us is very far from making human living simple and easy. On the contrary, it complicates matters, since it opens up possibilities for men and women that otherwise might be overlooked or neglected. It reveals that depths to which we humans may fall and the heights to which we may rise. And to speak of love both as the divine reality and as the clue to truly human existence is not to talk sentimentality or cheap emotionalism or easy toleration. Yet, as Sophocles in *Oedipus in Colonus* has the father say to the daughter, "One word frees us from all the weight and pain of life: that word is love." If a Greek tragedian could say this, surely a Christian who is committed to "the love of God in Christ Jesus our Lord" must affirm it all the more vigorously, with a deeper meaning and with stronger conviction—recognizing, at the same moment, that to say, really to mean, and to intend to live by such an affirmation takes all there is of him or her.

In respect, then, to the human concerns that occupy our attention in these chapters, becoming and belonging, as characteristic of love-in-action, will be emphasized. The context for the entire treatment will be a consistent and coherent worldview that in my belief is appropriate to the Christian tradition of faith, worship, and life and that at the same time can make sense to men and women today in their desire for a meaningful interpretation of their existence, of the world in which that existence is found, and of the divine reality we call God. And we can profit these days from a vigorous emphasis on God as "pure unbounded Love," to offset the all-too-frequent talk about deity in terms of sheer power or as a rigid moralist, not to mention the tendency to think of deity as the far-distant and unconcerned "first cause" of the world.

So what has Christian faith to tell us? First of all, God is seen as supremely Love-in-act. Since God is this, God must be in real, not merely logical, relation with the created order. God both gives and receives. And the clue to the divine nature is always to be found in the divine activity: "a thing is what it does," as Whitehead said in a different but not unconnected respect. If God is really actively engaged with and in the world, adapting the divine intention to it, taking into the divine life what occurs there, and hence seriously affected by it quite as much as sustaining it creatively and working within it to accomplish an enduring purpose, then indeed God must be understood in a fashion that is most suitably symbolized by what we know of relationship at the human level—granted, of course, that we say this with an *O altitudo*, to use Sir Thomas Browne's phrase. Thus, God transcends yet also undergirds the creation, works in it, and receives from it.

An extended quotation from Prof. Keith Ward's recent book, *Rational Theology and the Creativity of God*, is relevant here. He writes:

> We might think of God . . . as exercising three sorts of causality. . . . He posits a finite world, setting the powers of finite creatures, and thereby realizing new sorts of actual good, which modify his own states by his appreciation of them. . . . Then, in accordance with the necessary schema of all possible worlds and values . . . he sets the final goal of the world. He is the archetypal ideal which draws it towards the fullness of its distinctive perfection. One may thus see the world as an emergent autonomous unity, developing . . . partly at random and always influenced by the exemplary "Ideal," which itself is continually modified in detail as the world develops, to articulate it in more specific particularity. Finally, as God appreciates and responds to

his world, he plays a changing, modifying role within it, bringing creatures to share in his goodness in specific ways. His action [is] an immanent dynamic process, shaping and guiding events to actualize specific values, while allowing creaturely autonomy its proper exercise. This mode of divine action is modified both by individual characteristics in the finite world and by the sorts of response which sentient beings make to it. God continually and universally acts to shape many varied images of his own being out of what stands at the greatest remove from himself, without compromising the freedom of the creatures to build their own self-generated response to their vision of perfection. (pp. 222-33)

Probably Professor Ward would not call himself a Process philosopher or theologian, yet clearly his argument here is in close agreement with the Process understanding I am urging upon the reader. He is prepared to say, in the same discussion, that we can call God nothing other than "self-giving Love." What is more, he sees that to talk in the fashion in which he has done is intimately tied in with a picture of deity that is both biblically responsible and in accordance with what our contemporary knowledge has to tell us about the way things appear to us through observation and investigation.

If (as I like to do) we use Whiteheadian language, we properly make important distinctions when we speak of deity. We can say that, as *primordial,* God is the continuum of all possibilities, the treasure-house of potentiality to be applied to the creation; that, as *consequent* (or as affected by that creation), God is the recipient of all value of good achieved in the creative advance; and that, as *superjective,* God "pours back into the world" (as Whitehead once put it) that which has thus been received from it but is now harmonized within the divine life that is "the Harmony of harmonies."

In Charles Hartshorne's way of saying it, God is eternally and absolutely Love-in-act and is utterly faithful to righteous and caring purposes. Yet God in the concrete and divine existence is always related to the world in such a way that there is divine self-identification with and openness to affect from the world. God is committed to the creation and, therefore, cannot be taken as statically timeless but rather as eminently "time-full"—*from* the past, *in* the present, *toward* the future. And in accomplishing the divine purpose, there is complete respect for, and a valuing and employment of, the creation's own dignity and freedom, its responsibility for decisions, and its capacity to act as a genuine cause in the total advance.

God is disclosed in some degree or manner everywhere throughout the creation, and this is always in terms of the divine activity or what God is *doing* with it, for it, and in it. But there are some points or places where there may be a more "important" disclosure. The creation is not "uniformitarian" but varied, aesthetically contrasting the *now* with the *then,* the *here* with the *there.* In this fashion, a particular event or occasion may be taken as our best clue to or symbol of what, so to say, God is "up to" all the time and everywhere. And God is both active *and* passive; he or she initiates possibility, lures towards realization, and is therefore "modified" (as Keith Ward puts it) by that movement and its results. God both acts and is acted upon, a position that much "classical theism" has refused to take. But since this is the case with God, we can speak meaningfully of a divine enrichment by accomplished good in creation, and we can also allow for what might be styled a divine sadness because of wrong creaturely decisions and what they bring about. God shares in the anguish of the world; God suffers with the world without being overcome by the wrong in it: in Whitehead's fine phrase, God is "the fellow-sufferer who understands."

Second, the basic significance of the creation is to be found in its contribution to the divine life, for the enrichment of that life. The world has its own integrity, its own capacity to act causatively, its own creative power; it is not like a puppet that God pulls by a string. Yet it is open to the divine action upon it, and thanks to that action and its own creativity, it may move toward its own proper good and thus find self-fulfillment. Hence, God's purpose for the creature and the creature's self-realization are not contradictory one of the other; they are different ways of seeing and speaking about the same enterprise. God's inescapable "secular function" is precisely here: guiding, luring, and attracting. Thus, the initiating possibility can become a genuine actualization. Nor is this confined to the human or historical level, as some theologies seem to assume, but is found everywhere, although obviously not always recognized and named for what it is. In a word, the divine activity is cosmic in scope, including in its concern the natural order and what goes on there.

In the third place, human existence (about which we shall have much more to say at a later stage) is itself a creaturely movement intended to reflect and serve instrumentally for the divine goodness. To move toward actualizing human possibility, in full integrity of body, mind, will, affection, and always in social belonging, *is* to become human. To fall away from it is to fail the human goal and at the same time to fail the cosmic process and the God who is the basic thrust or drive in that process. Our deepest human problem is to know and use, through decision, this capacity to develop toward fulfillment. Our deepest human tragedy is that easily attainable ends and a self-centered achievement may be chosen by us. Then human existence is frustrated, trivialized, and degraded. What is more, the fact of our human sociality is such that wrongness in one place infects the whole enterprise, just as rightness has its wide influence and its good consequences for others of our race. Something of the same sort may be said, by analogy, of other ranges of the creation.

Lastly, evil—which will be discussed at some length in the next chapter—is a reality we humans all experience, observe, and do. Yet it is not willed by God, either directly or permissively, as if things might have been otherwise, but God allows evil to happen. Only insofar as there is a world at all, with its necessary freedom, can God be said thus to be responsible. But God's limitation, as Whitehead and Charles Hartshorne have insisted, is sheer goodness. In that goodness God grants freedom to the creation, with the result that decisions, conscious or unconscious, may and in fact do produce evil that God neither wills nor wants. We cannot be cheerfully optimistic about the world or about ourselves; neither need we be entirely pessimistic, as if nothing could be done about the matter. Instead, we should be realistic, facing the fact of evil in all its forms but ready also to see that the infinite resourcefulness of the divine Love-in-act can find ways of handling such evil, so that a positive good may result in the end. We humans are invited to join in the struggle to overcome evil and to further good. About this more will also be said in the chapter that follows.

Perhaps I have indicated sufficiently how a Christian Process Theology sees God, the world, and human existence. Let us now turn to some specifically Christian affirmations, and here I must be selective since far too many aspects of Christian faith might be discussed. I have chosen for first attention the area known as Christology: "the doctrine of Christ," as it is called in theological textbooks. I shall then say something again about human existence in the light of Christology; and I shall conclude with the question of human destiny. I hope that what is said about these topics will illustrate the fashion in which other aspects of Christian thought would be handled by one who accepts the Process way of seeing things.

We can have no doubt that in Christian faith the event of Jesus Christ is central and decisive. As Whitehead once put it, "Buddhism and Christianity find their origins in two inspired moments of history, the life of the Buddha and the life of Christ. The Buddha gave his doctrine to enlighten the world; Christ gave his life. It is for Christians to discern the doctrine" (*Religion in the Making*, p. 55). Unquestionably, Whitehead was right in this observation, and a large part of Christian theology has sought to do precisely this: "discern the doctrine." But the fact of the event comes first.

It is frequently said that Christianity is "a historical religion." In one sense this is certainly true since it comes to us through a long historical tradition or social process whose origin is found in something that is believed to have happened factually in the distant past. On the other hand, if "historical" implies that we possess material that gives us an entirely accurate and completely reliable account of the life and work of Jesus, such as we might have about Julius Caesar or Napoleon, it is an inexact and misleading phrase. After a long period of literary, historical, and form-critical study of the New Testament, along with more recent work on the "redaction" of its several books in the light of the motives that led their authors to select and arrange the material then available to them, it is clear that any claim to "simple historicity" is false.

Whitehead was no biblical scholar, but he noted, in the same context as the quotation I have just given from him, that "we do not possess a systematic detailed record of the life of Christ." He went on to say that what we *do* possess is "a peculiarly vivid record of the first response to it in the minds of the first group of disciples after the lapse of some years, with their recollections, interpretations, and incipient formulations." That is to say, we have in the New Testament a very early—almost a primitive—witness to the impact or impression made by Jesus Christ. This is a witness that is given to us "from faith to faith"—from the faith of those who in early days committed themselves in response to it and with the intention of awakening faith in others.

In a recent essay by Leslie Houlden, which appears in the symposium *Alternative Approaches to New Testament Study* (edited by A.E. Harvey), the point is well made:

> It is an over-simplification, yet far from being a falsehood or a gross distortion, to say that the Christian faith began with the impact of the career of Jesus (whether perceived as a whole or in terms of some part of it). . . . The fact of substantial immediate impact, unrivalled among Jewish contemporaries who can be put forward for comparison, is undeniable. . . . What is available to us as wholly incontrovertible and objective is . . . the *fact* of his impact. (p. 134)

Houlden goes on to tell us that there is diversity in the reporting of how this impact occurred; yet he rejects the claim, sometimes made by highly skeptical scholars, "that no intelligible picture can emerge and no statement, of greater or lesser probability, concerning the Jesus whose impact those who gave the early witness experienced, can be made" (p. 134).

If fundamentalist Christians look at the scriptural material as generally inerrant, many more liberal Christians have all too often thought that by proper analysis it is possible to acquire information about the so-called Jesus of history and then to speak with confidence about what he said and did and even about what he believed about himself and his vocation. But this will not really do. Everything that we "know" about Jesus comes to us through the apostolic witness, as this has been handed down in the living tradition of the Christian community of faith, worship, and life. The New Testament is part of that tradition, not separated from it; therefore, its significance is in reporting the earliest ways, so far as we can recover them, in which Jesus was understood by men and women who themselves were caught up in that tradition and who found (as Houlden notes) "an experience of salvation, of new well-being in relation to God" in their response to the event about which the witness spoke (p. 135). In the community that "remembered Jesus," to use John Knox's phrase, the primitive experience found that this same Jesus was made available to them "in the Spirit," which animated the fellowship and which seemed to them decisive for human existence under God.

There is also a further point to be made here. This has to do with what nowadays is styled the cultural relativism that marks any report of events in the past. Far too frequently an appeal is made to some biblical passage or series of passages, or to ancient Christian thinkers, as if this would readily settle whatever question is under discussion. But we must recognize that a difference of outlook makes our own situation unlike that of any given period in the past. Even in the Bible itself there is an enormous diversity of view so that no single position can be called "biblical" without qualification. Here some words of Leonard Hodgson are worth quoting: "As one who has been a professional teacher of theology for forty years, I now publicly declare my hope that no pupil of mine will ever be guilty of using the expression 'The Bible says' " (*For Faith and Freedom*, vol. 2, p. 12). With respect also to earlier Christian thinkers and their various statements, there is Hodgson's further remark—which those of us who were his students vividly recall—that we must always ask something like this: "What must the truth be for us *now*, if people like that"—he was referring both to biblical writers and theologians in the past history of the Church—"put it in the way they did?" Here as everywhere Hodgson's honesty was apparent. He saw that "new occasions" not only "teach new duties" but that they also "make ancient good uncouth" and that our responsibility, granted the relativism that attaches to all our experience and our statement, is to think afresh, on the basis of the general apostolic witness and with due regard for earlier Christian teaching, as well as in the light of our own experience of "newness of life," so that what we have to say is *nove* (newly said) and often is also *nova* (the saying of new things). I am using here the famous words of Vincent of Lerins, a Christian scholar of the early Church. Only by this sort of approach can we hope to be faithful to the living tradition that by that very "aliveness" makes archaeological theologizing incredible and intolerable. Like every social process, the Christian community has its own identity in the direction or routing that it takes from the past, in the present, and toward the future; but we dare not stop it, if we could, at some given point that happens to be attractive to us with our own special predilections and prejudices.

However, recognition of this inescapable relativism does not mean that we have *no* grounds for a faith that is in genuine continuity with what has gone before. By what Whitehead styled "the appeal to the direct intuition of special occasions—" he was referring to the primitive days of the Church in which Jesus' impact was known as a reality—we may possess, and Christian conviction affirms that we do possess, a key or clue "of universal validity, to be applied by faith to the ordering of all experience." What this signifies for Christian theology is the need to produce *some* formulation ("doctrine"); but the important thing is not the exact details of such formulations, nor even the formulations themselves, but the reality with which they seek to deal. The definitions, whatever they may be, are inevitably tied in with the worldview they presuppose. Changing circumstances, new conditions, and differing ways of seeing things are a fact; they require of us some attempt at reconception. For a "dogma," in the sense of a precise statement or formulation, can never be final; it can only be "adequate" to the period in which it has been worked out. On the other hand, as Whitehead went on to say, "the great instantaneous conviction behind the dogma" is indeed the "good news or gospel" that is basic to the community's identity, and the community is enabled "to maintain its integrity by its recurrence to the inspired simplicity of its origin."

How then can we today interpret this event we indicate when we say "Jesus"? First, it is imperative for us to see the originating event in its totality: to study the preparation for it reported in the Old Testament, which sums up Jewish religious conviction in all its diversity and complexity; to note what the early witness tells us about the person at its center and how that person was "received"; and to discern what has happened in consequence during succeeding centuries. In this totality there is, of course, included the story of Jesus' remembered teaching, acts, and relationships, as well as his death and the way in which through death he was believed to have been "let loose into the world" (as John Masefield once put it) as he was also believed to have been "raised from the dead" and received by God into the divine life. For Christian faith there is here "the supreme moment in history," as Whitehead said. Nowhere has this been more beautifully described than by Whitehead in the passage quoted earlier:

The essence of Christianity is the appeal to the life of Christ as a revelation of the nature of God and of his agency in the world. The record is fragmentary, inconsistent, and uncertain. . . . But there can be no doubt as to what elements in the record have evoked a response from all that is best in human nature: the mother, the Child, and the bare manger: the lowly man, homeless and self-forgetful, with his message of peace, love, and sympathy: the suffering,

12

the agony, the tender words as life ebbed, the final despair: and the whole with the authority of supreme victory. (*Adventure in Ideas,* pp. 170-71)

We observed that Whitehead went on to ask, "Can there be any doubt that the power of Christianity lies in its revelation in act, of that which Plato divined in theory?" And what did Plato—and many others in various religions and cultures, each in his or her own fashion—thus "divine in theory"? The answer is plain, and Whitehead phrases it simply: "The divine element in the world is to be conceived as a persuasive agency and not as a coercive agency." In other words, the basic insight of Christian faith, in the context of the other world religions, is that "God is Love," Love active in creation and Love the essential character of God.

What is known as Christology is the effort to make sense of all this, not in abstraction from the experience of Christian people but as a consequence of that continuing experience. In the past this task has been undertaken by way of talk about two "substances" (one divine, one human) united in "one person" or talk about two wills (again one divine and one human) in one person or talk about two "consciousnesses" thus united. Over the years such talk seems to me to have shown its inadequacy and indeed its impossibility for us. I urge that our best approach is to take with great seriousness the primacy and centrality of love—in this case, God's prevenient or initiative Love as this is responded to in obedient human love. When Theodore of Mopsuestia, an Antiochene theologian in the age of the Christian Fathers, spoke of *sunapheia* (or deep union) and *eudokia* (or divine goodwill) as helping us here, he was right. These provide a clue to the way in which Jesus Christ may be interpreted as that One in whom God's activity in Love and as Love *and* a genuine responsive human movement in love were brought together in a union that was neither incidental nor accidental but enduring.

Yet we need to remember that such a position cannot be *demonstrated* by appeal to this or that detail of Jesus' life, since we do not have the information that would make

13

that appeal valid. What *can* be done, however, is to refer to the early apostolic witness, seen in the context of the living Christian tradition, and to the manner in which that witness stressed both the centrality of the figure of Jesus and the enormous impact he had made. The conclusion of the matter is plainly stated in 1 John: "Herein is love, not that we loved God but that he loved us, and sent his Son that we might live through him."

I now turn to speak fairly briefly about what it means to be human, although in later chapters this will be discussed at length. We have seen that each of us is a living process, not a static "it" that was once created and now continues without change. Each of us is a "becoming" whose existence is toward making actual the initial possibilities given to us; we move toward, or away from, that realization. Each of us is a particular "himself" or "herself." Compounded of body, mind, emotion, and possessed of a striving after goals, we are grasped by, and we grasp, one or other of the many lures that come to us; we make our decisions, often insignificant but sometimes very decisive. We are a "becoming," we are also a "belonging," since we share in the common human life—"no man is an island entire unto itself," said John Donne in a famous passage—and what we decide affects others and also affects God. Our human possibility, therefore, is to move toward "the image of God" who is Love-in-act. Hence, we are to become "lovers-in-the-making" in all our shared finitude, obvious mortality, and patent defectiveness.

We share also in the accumulated wrong in our world, not only through our own wrong choices but because we inherit a distorted situation thanks to millenia of wrong choices in the history of which we are part. Our moral judgments, both in respect to ourselves and to others, must therefore be made in terms of the general direction in which we are moving. The significance of particular incidents is to be found in their indication of that direction, whether toward true humanness or toward a debasing of our humanity. God treats us as sons and daughters, providing attractions from his or her circumambient love and usually under creaturely incognitos (including above all our fellow humans), which can save us from ourselves and set us on the path toward fuller shared existence here and now, with the promise that our achievements, when they are for good, will be received by God. When they are not for good they may still be taken by God and be transformed into occasions for the better. But we dare not "run to Daddy" to set things right when, through our own errors and wrongdoings, things have gone badly. God "redeems us" but not by denying our own freedom and accountability. Redemption is by God's taking us now for what we have it in us to become and for what (through our commitment in faith in that same God) is already intimated and even experienced in some degree.

Finally, we may ask about human destiny. In the Process conceptuality, as also in the biblical material, God is seen as affected by what happens in the creation. What happens makes a difference *to* God and *in* God, although God remains always the supreme, worshipful, dependable, and unsurpassable one, "than whom nothing greater can be conceived." Once received by God, no accomplished good can be "lost." Charles Hartshorne has spoken of "the divine memory" as unfailing both in its retention and in its employment of what has been received. This is "objective immortality," in Whitehead's phrasing; by virtue of it, creaturely "perishing" does not mean total annihilation but rather participation in the divine existence. All this can be seen as a valid Christian interpretation of our destiny as men and women.

But is such participation also "subjective," so that the human agent has a concious awareness of it? Here there is a difference of opinion among Process theologians. Many would affirm some sort of subjective immortality; others would say that subjective immortality, while conceivable, is not a requirement of Christian faith. I agree with the latter group because I take seriously the theocentrism or "God-centeredness" of that faith and the obvious fact of human finitude. Yet, on the other hand, for a Christian, death cannot mean the "total annihilation" mentioned above. It does indeed mark the end of our finite existence; but it is an end that has its terminus *in God*, and hence it cannot be utter annihilation. If God receives and remembers, infallibly and unfailingly, nothing is really "lost"; it persists in God who is never lost. Achieved good, accomplished justice, truth in its fullness: all these are forever "safe" in God, to whom alone (as a biblical text puts it) belongs immortality. Whatever that may include, all is *ad dei gloriam*—in the deepest sense of those splendid Latin words.

In a recent book (*After Death: Life in God,* SCM Press) I have argued that what has just been said is a proper "demythologizing" of traditional Christian talk about death, judgment, resurrection, and eternal life. I have also urged that all these have their existential significance for our living here and now. In any event, we need to remember the saying of St. Francis de Sales: "We are to seek the God of consolations, not the consolations of God." To be "raised" from death into the life of God is the glorious fulfillment of all human aspiration, struggle, and desire, both for ourselves and for those whom we hold dear.

2

The Loving God and the Fact of Evil

We live in a world where the reality of evil—of various sorts, such as natural disorder, animal suffering, human pain and accident, and moral wrong as well as sin—is an inescapable fact. Of course, at times this is not vividly experienced. Most of us, most of the time, probably manage to live a reasonably happy life and avoid dwelling on what is wrong in the creation. But there are also the moments of tragedy—someone we love dies of cancer, there is an appalling airplane crash, we hear about a devastating earthquake or a tidal wave, famine strikes some part of the world—when any man or woman who is at all sensitive will admit that this is not "a nice world" but rather is filled with tragedy, sadness, and pain. What is more, we humans are selfish, lustful, destructive, and careless of our human sisters and brothers much of the time if not all of the time. And to some the most dreadful aspect is the spectacle called by Tennyson "nature red in tooth and claw," when it seems that the animal kingdom is marked by shocking cruelty and suffering.

A discussion of evil is essential at this point in our discussion. For if we believe in God, we must somehow reconcile these appalling facts with the belief that God is good and caring. Only so can we make sense of the world and of ourselves in that world. Hence, we face the question, Why is there evil in the world and in human experience? In this chapter we are looking at the fact of evil from a specifically Christian perspective, and no Christian can be like the ostrich, which is said to bury its head in the sand when a storm sweeps over the desert. But if there is anything to say that will assist us to deal with this question, it can only be entertained if first we look honestly at the facts. As Thomas Hardy once put it,

> If way to the better there be
> It exacts a full look at the worst.

As it happens, authentic Christian faith throughout the centuries has sought to do just this, but often with indifferent success. Why is this?

I believe that much of the time the chief difficulty is with the "model" or concept of God that Christians have taken to be right, when it is not only inadequate but actually mistaken. Earlier in this book I have discussed those errors, noting what Whitehead had to say about what he styled "the apostasy" of much Christian theism, with its talk about deity as like a "despotic ruler" who is in complete control of everything that happens in the creation and, hence, must be responsible for all that takes place within it. In an older day, insurance policies used to express this idea when they spoke about natural catastrophes and other such happenings as "acts of God." Ordinary men and women seem often to think of God as callously inflicting evil or as indifferent to what goes on in the world. I need not repeat here what has already been said about a genuinely Christian picture of God, in contrast to these and other notions. I only insist again that if the great central Christian affirmation is indeed that the clue to God's "nature and activity" is the event of Jesus Christ, then it is imperative to see and say that "God is Love" and that God never acts in such a fashion that deity may correctly be regarded as responsible directly or even permissively (save in there being a world at all) for anything and everything that takes place in the creation. God's nature and God's activity are always caring and loving, persuading and luring, never sheerly coercive and never imposed arbitrarily on that creation.

In a sense, however, this conviction makes the fact of evil all the more inexplicable and puzzling. But here it is important to recognize that a corollary of this conception of

God as "sheer Love," and as always acting lovingly, is that the creation has its freedom, its causative capacity, and its necessary accountability for what occurs in that freedom. Hence, the world is not some sort of object that God shoves around, intrudes into, and manipulates. To the contrary, it is there as a given fact with its specific characteristics that God respects and with which God deals.

Perhaps this can best be exemplified by what we know in our own experience. In our relationships with others, when those relationships are fully human, there is always the granting to the "other" the right to decide whether or not, and how, that "other" will respond to our attitude and action toward her or him. The relationship presupposes a personal kind of activity and attitude that will be expressed in various ways but never through sheer force or coercion exercised by one upon the other. Now what is true in our experience at the human level is also true, in appropriate fashion, of God's way in the world. The insurance policy's notion that "act of God" means something else is entirely mistaken—mistaken, that is, if the "brief Galilean vision" is our best intimation of God. Indeed, the most patent manifestation of an "act of God," a Christian should insist, is a particular human existence in which rationality, imagination, respect, moral integrity, and the like were most present and visible. The ancient Christian thinker Irenaeus of Lyons once said that "the glory of God is man fully alive." This is the way in which a Christian can understand Jesus Christ as "an act of God," and similarly, it provides a clue to how God may be taken to act in every range of the creation. God respects and uses the creaturely status of each element in the world and, indeed, of the world altogether.

Thus, God is not arbitrary power acting immediately upon the world, as it were, without any mediation, controlling everything in it and, hence, directly responsible for what takes place. That is an idea that is associated with ancient tyrannies and despotisms and is fallacious when applied to God's relationship with the creation. Nor is God unaffected by what goes on in the world; rather, what happens there matters to God and makes a difference for and to God. In such a context, the world has its own independence, its own freedom, and its own accountability. As I have said, we can see this vividly as a matter of human experience, and we can legitimately generalize from that human level, taking it as indicative (however remotely) of what is going on everywhere and always.

At the level of strictly natural existence, as also in inanimate nature, such qualities are not obviously observable. Yet we know nowadays that human existence has emerged from and is a part of the total "natural world." Therefore, that world can be properly interpreted only when we begin where we are, in human life with its relative independence, freedom, and accountability. Far too often in the past and far too frequently even today, thinkers have argued the other way on; they have assumed that human existence can be understood only in terms of the nonhuman. The result has been disastrous. It is the explanation of much that is wrong in human living. Perhaps the ancients had some excuse when they thought in this fashion; for us today, with our awareness of an evolutionary creation, there is no excuse to continue in so mistaken a fashion. We might even say that awareness of just that evolutionary creation has been a blessing and not (as some seem to feel) a dreadful curse.

Hence, it is necessary to reconceive some ancient beliefs. Omnipotence does not mean God's sheer existence as "almighty power" without qualification. Omniscience and omnipresence can also be given a different meaning. *Omnipotence* is the strength of the divine Love-in-act in a world that (as I have said again and again) possesses its own independence and freedom. *Omniscience* means that Love, God as Love, is all-knowing about what in fact happens and of the various possibilities that the creation may actualize— but without dictating them. *Omnipresence* tells us that the divine Love is everywhere and always present and at work to augment the good, often in very surprising places—a Christian would point especially to a humble human life, to a man born in a manger, and to that same man rejected and put to death, as the place where such active presentness is most clearly seen.

Does this signify that God is "finite" or "limited"? *Only* if we have begun with the presumption that what is ultimate

20

must be sheer coercive power and control. But God is not "finite," if it is true that Love is the ultimate reality, as a Christian who knows his or her business ought to maintain. Nor is God "limited," excepting insofar as Love cannot— literally *cannot*, being Love—control everything but must wait for some such response to its prior invitation as may be found, in differing ways and with most varying intensity, in the world that is ours *and God's*. The response at the natural level and at the so-called "animal level" may be minimal. Yet it is there when, for example, an electron "decides"—that is to say, "cuts off" (which is what *decide* means etymologically) one available possibility by adopting another. Modern quantum theory, the "uncertaincy principle," and "particle physics" demonstrate this genuine openness. Of course, there is no conscious choice at such points, but experience precedes consciousness, which is a fairly high level of such experience. And so up the scale, through more complex natural phenomena, until at the human level (with its obvious independence and accountability) freedom is grasped in a conscious experience.

We often call things "natural evils": hurricanes, earthquakes, and tidal waves; in animal life, the struggle for existence among and within species, but never with the *intentional* inflicting of pain, since at that level there can be little if any real intentionality as we understand it in ourselves; and with us humans the horror of sheer self-centeredness, neglect of or hatred for others, the inflicting of pain, injustice, and oppression, with all that these bring about. Such occurrences show vividly and clearly what can go wrong. Our world is not "predestinated" in this way or that. It is not regulated by "laws which never shall be broken," save only by the basic law of inevitable consequences for what is done, whether for good or for ill. As modern scientists increasingly stress, it is an "open world," where choices make a difference and where that difference has its results in the continuing "ongoing." In such a world, God cannot be held responsible for what we, or any other element or aspect of the creation, choose to do. God accepts the facts for what they are, given this relative creaturely freedom, and God deals with these facts as they are. The divine purpose is the wider and more inclusive working of "Love-in-act," or God, with a responsive love from the creaturely side. Furthermore, as St. Paul puts it in Rom. 8:28, "God works in every respect towards a good end"; God calls us to be (in Whitehead's fine words) "co-creators" in the creative advance.

Having said all this, it is now proper for us to suggest what might be styled "ameliorating considerations." However black the picture may be as we look at it, there is something to be said on the other side.

First of all, this world was not "created" exactly as we now see it, in a single, all-at-once act. Thanks to evolutionary science we know that it is a world in which for untold millenia creation there has been, still is, and will continue to be a process or development. In a way, we might say that it resembles a place where an artisan is engaged in making something or other; there are loose ends here and there, bits and pieces that are not yet completed, remnants of earlier efforts that did not quite fulfill the artisan's plan. Ours is an "unfinished world," as somebody has put it. We cannot expect, if that is true, to find everything perfectly accomplished. On the contrary, what we are bound to find is a continuing work in which the aim is to create something splendid and beautiful—but that final aim is not yet achieved. In Christian thought and in biblical writing, there is talk of *eschatology,* or a future-to-be-realized one day. Doubtless the biblical material on the subject is in highly metaphorical, poetic, or (if you will) mythological language. Such language is natural to all religious discourse. We cannot talk literally about matters like that because we cannot penetrate into the divine nature, purpose, and goal. Nonetheless, the material helps us to see that "there is more to come," and Christian faith would insist that *God* is actively engaged in working toward that end, not remote from and unconcerned with what takes place, but genuinely and vigorously acting toward it and in it with respect for and use of creaturely freedom and accountability.

Second, a considerable part of "natural evil" is called that only when and as human life is involved. A tidal wave that devastates an uninhabited island in the South Pacific is not usually called evil. But when men and women suffer from the results of the wave, we are more likely to call it evil. Furthermore, a good deal that takes place in the natural order is tied in with providing what L.J. Henderson, the Harvard scientists, once called "the fitness of the environment," in which conditions are maintained that make possible human existence now and in the future. Without at least some such happenings, human life on this planet would long since have disappeared.

In the third place, there is, as I have already said, no *intentional* inflicting of evil in most if not all suffering in the animal world. Unlike humans, who can and often do set out to make others suffer, animals are primarily concerned to "protect their territory," as students of their behavior tell us, or to save their young from attack, or to secure necessary supplies of food for their survival. If these experts are to be trusted—and I here recall a world-famous biologist with whom I once talked—the actual suffering in the animal world is much less severe than it seems to us to be. We tend to project our own sensitivity here, said this friend, who went on to tell me (to my surprise) that when a crab tears away the claw of another crab, as I had reported to him, the probability is that what the latter feels is more like a twinge than like the anguish that the tearing away of a limb would cause in us. Incidently, this did not lead my friend to say that there is *no* pain there but only that we should not commit the "pathetic fallacy" of reading our own feeling-tones into the animal world. At the same time, he insisted that it is quite wrong for us to inflict *any* unnecessary suffering on animals—which was why he opposed "blood sports," although he was not a vegetarian.

Fourth, in a world where things can and often do go wrong, it is not surprising that, for example, parasites thrive on their "host" and, therefore, damage and even destroy that upon which they depend. Sometimes the suffering caused in this fashion (as with malignant cancerous growth) has its ultimate origin in some human misuse, bad diet or infection or lack, again without malicious intent on the part of the agent that causes it. Furthermore, we need to recognize the plain fact that a good deal of physical and, even more obviously, of psychological suffering is made possible through exactly the same human (and other) conditioning that makes it possible to enjoy the sense of well-being, even of joy, that marks most of human (and, in an analagous fashion, animal) existence. We should be careful in our approach. For we could not "feel pain," but neither could we "feel happiness," if we did not have such psycho-physical equipment. Laughter and tears are intimately related, as folk wisdom knows and as many poets have told us. It is also the case that our human solidarity, our participation in a common life, and our intimacy with others occasion much of the suffering that we experience. When a friend suffers, especially if that person is one for whom we care deeply, the anguish can be enormous. This we all know, yet frequently we do not take it into account when we speak of various sorts of human suffering.

I shall not discuss in detail the question of moral evil, nor shall I speak of what in religious language is called "sin." These topics are far too big to receive here the attention they deserve. But it must be said that moral evil and sin are tied in with the very freedom and responsibility that men and women know and value. They are the result of our relatively free moral decisions or they are caused by the social situation in which we men and women inevitably find ourselves. We are often accountable for them; no fully human person is likely to blame somebody or something else for all of them. In one sense however we are *all* "accountable" here, because we belong to a society of humans that is often based upon, or that creates, injustice, oppression, servitude, and other unhappy aspects of the world. In two other books I have discussed these at some length: *Goodness Distorted* (London: Mowbrays, 1970) and *Cosmic Love and Human Wrong* (New York: Paulist Press, 1978); perhaps I may refer the reader to them for a fuller treatment of moral evil and sin.

The several points that have just been made as "ameliorating considerations" do not *reduce* the reality of evil. However, they help us to avoid the totally pessimistic interpretation that can easily be mistaken for genuine realism in understanding. Or, to use again Hardy's words, there is a "better" as there is a "worst." Total gloom is just as unrealistic as bland optimism. And on the whole, most of human and animal life is enjoyed, and the living of it gives considerable satisfaction.

Now we return to the earlier question about God's nature and point out that deity is not unrelated to, nor unaffected by, the creation in which God is active. We can affirm that the exercise of "power" in that divine working is only for maintaining a cosmos or an orderly pattern rather than allowing the world to fall into chaotic or anarchic confusion. But throughout, God is deeply concerned for it. For relationship *is* concern, whether positive or negative. What God does *positively* is to labor toward richer, fuller, more inclusive, expanding existence; *negatively* God acts against the evil that may be there, and by what might be styled "the divine alchemy" God seems able to "bring good out of evil"—although this is no excuse for the doing of evil so that good may come in the end. Such an attitude would be alien to the whole picture that we have here sought to present about God's ways with the creation.

God *is* Love—and this is an *active* Love. "A thing is what it does," I have quoted from Whitehead. Active and concerned loving always seeks to identify itself with the beloved; it cannot remain aloof but must participate, so far as possible, in the beloved's pains and difficulties quite as much as in his or her joys and happiness. This is precisely what Christians have said about God when they have taken seriously the faith that God is disclosed, enacted, expressed, or "incarnate" in the total event of Jesus Christ. In that event, with a distinctive clarity, God is seen to be actively present, to have made himself or herself one with, and thus genuinely a sharer in, creaturely existence at our human level. This conviction may then be taken as a clue for the reading of *all* that God does. Then God will be seen as a suffering God who shares in the anguish of the creation yet is not overcome or destroyed by that sharing. For a corollary of the Christian conviction is that divine Love, enacted in this human existence, was not defeated by the death that is part of the creaturely lot. The various stories that tell of Jesus' "resurrection," when suitably "demythologized,"

25

tell us that Love expressed in the world, sharing in the world's pain, and knowing from "inside" its anguish, "cannot be holden of death," as the New Testament phrases it. The reports about that "resurrection" cannot easily be reconciled to make a consistent narrative. Yet the fact of the disciples' awareness that Jesus, in the totality of his existence, was victorious is plain to see; God "raised him from the dead."

God is "the fellow-sufferer who understands," in Whitehead's fine phrase. But God does more than "understand"; God is in the world, knowing it from the inside and not merely as an external observer who deeply sympathizes. Of course, Whitehead meant that, too. God is actively engaged in overcoming evil, in all its differing modes. The divine aim or purpose, in a world that has its own independence and freedom, is precisely to overcome evil. But that is not done in one fell swoop; it can only be done by a continuing and persistent effort on God's part. And there is a consequence for us.

What is that consequence? I have stressed that we are called as humans to be what St. Paul styled "fellow-workers with God." We are to work with God in furthering the creative advance of the world in goodness, truth, justice, righteousness, care, and love. Such is the practical Christian vocation. Therefore, our Christian attitude toward whatever is evil is a firm rejection of it and an earnest effort against it, to the end that it shall be overcome, negated, removed from the world or transformed into an occasion for good to emerge.

Of course, we can do little if anything against natural disaster; we cannot remove or defeat tidal waves or earthquakes, although we can see to it that people do not live in places where these are likely to occur. We can do something to alleviate pain in the animal world, if only by refusing to inflict suffering beyond absolute necessity. We can work against illness and disease, by the use of such knowledge and techniques as are acquired through the study of those ills. Above all, we can open ourselves to the forces for good that are present in the world, so that human self-centeredness, cruelty to one's fellows, oppression, hatred, and contempt shall not prevail among us. This is the challenge to us in our Christian discipleship.

When the day comes for judgment upon our loyalty and dedication, God will ask us (or so we might put it) the question that was put by the captain in the Hundred Years War when he came upon a soldier who had skulked in his tent while the fierce struggle was going on: "When we fought at Arles, were *you* there?" If we were not there, in that continuing struggle for the good, we have shown ourselves to be unprofitable servants. We have been judged, and at our best we judge ourselves, to be unworthy of our "high calling in Christ Jesus our Lord." Even if there is no simple, straightforward, and easy explanation of evil, the obligation is laid upon us to work with God against it. The depth of Christian faith is to see, with Mother Julian of Norwich, that in and with God "all shall be well and all manner of thing shall be well." However, this conviction can be entertained meaningfully and realistically only if first of all we have recognized evil and have played our part in God's suffering, yet triumphant, activity against it.

Finally, do our liturgy and teaching express vividly this reality of God as Love-in-action and ourselves as God's agents in active loving? Anything that denies or minimizes that basic reality should have no place in our worship, our prayer, or our meditation. Fortunately, most of the newer services found in the recently revised service books of many Christian groups are in this sense more deeply Christian than earlier services. Surely it is necessary to eradicate from our theology whatever would suggest that God is in control of everything, exactly as it happens, and hence is fully responsible for what is wrong. Here much remains to be done; yet there are encouraging signs that Christian theologians are at work on this task, and we may hope that a more genuinely Christian theology may be the result of their labors. Our discipleship, which often has tended to be moralistic in a legal sense, also needs to be reconceived so that love has the preeminence, rather than the coldly moralistic interpretations of the divine purpose so often taught in the past and even today hanging on in many supposedly Christian circles. Here there is much still to be done.

For any genuinely dedicated Christian, faith and practice, worship and work, go hand in hand. Despite our ignorance of much that we might like to know and with an honest recognition that we do not and cannot "have all the answers to all the questions," we yet have enough to impel us to be responsible and zealous in thought and word and deed. As a distinguished English divine of an earlier generation once put it, Christian "faith is not belief in spite of evidence, but life in scorn of consequence." In fact, that faith is itself a call to action, and part of the action is for us to serve as God's agents in overcoming evil wherever we see it and to work with God and with our fellow humans so that the divine purpose of God for creation may be more effectively realized.

3

The Human Person

None of us can live to, of, and for self alone. To be human is not only to "become" but also to "belong"—to belong with other people, sharing with them in the human situation, participating in their interests, receiving from them and giving to them. This is why talk about ourselves as "individuals" is misleading; we are not so much individuals as *persons*. The dictionary definition of *individual* is "one instance of a class, species, or type"; no mention is made of relationships. But the word *person* suggests—or ought to suggest, if we have regard for the historical development of its usage—just such relationships, contexts, and setting. When people speak of individuals, they usually imply a stress on the self alone, almost, if not always, in isolation or separation from others. When they speak of persons, they imply the notion of social belonging in which men and women are so related that one might very well say that personality and sociality are two sides of the same coin, two aspects of the same reality.

In this chapter we shall begin with exactly those ideas, first with reference to ourselves. Then the next chapter will be a consideration of the one other to whom we are most intimately related, be it wife or lover or husband or very close friend. After that we shall look at wider relationships, first with the family and then with neighbors. Finally, we shall discuss the "city," or the broad and inclusive social group to which we belong. The purpose throughout will be to arrive at some understanding of what human becoming and belonging signify. It is natural that we start with our own self-awareness as this or that person. Yet we cannot remain there because (as I have urged) our specific human identity is largely dependent upon where we are, with another and with others and in genuine rapport with the human world as a whole.

I have just been speaking about our belonging; but we must also remember that to be human is to be becoming something or other. That is of first importance since in our self-awareness we do not feel as if we were "finished articles" but know that we are "on the move." This fact of our experience is not always given the attention it deserves, and many times descriptions of humankind are produced that suggest a quasi-morphological portrayal, as if human existence were like counting the spots on some insect or were like a diagram of a dead cat as it is studied in a biological laboratory. This sort of description may have value in certain scientific contexts, but if taken by itself it can be radically false.

We have seen that the world in which we exist is itself a matter of becoming and belonging. The evolutionary nature of things is plain enough; so is its societal quality. Evolution in this sense is no longer a matter of opinion, despite the crazy program of the so-called creationists in the United States. Evolution is an established fact about the world. Obviously the sort of change and the time span in which such change takes place varies from level to level—a rock does not change in the same fashion as an animal does. But it would be wrong to think that this denies change, just as it would be absurd to assume that everything "moves" in a manner identical with everything else. Still, general principles can be applied as widely as our knowledge goes; I have already made suggestions about such principles.

Now in a world like that, the ultimate constituents are events and not "substantial entities" to which predicates may then be attached if we wish to do so. The reality *is* the process: that is the point of the title of Whitehead's Gifford lectures, *Process and Reality.* Ordinary observation by a beholder might seem to give us a different picture. We speak of *this table* at which I am now sitting. Yet any informed

30

person knows that the table is an astonishingly complex mass of whirling bits of energy or moments of activity. Its hardness and permanence are in one sense an illusion; to speak of them is convenient and important in some respects but misleading in the last analysis. In one sense, too, each of *us* has an identity; but that is to be found in a series of routings of events and experiences that are held together in some sort of unity of direction. These can appear to give us both permanence and some sort of fixity. There certainly *is* the identity; but it is not the kind that depends upon absolute changelessness.

In the world as we now know it to be, all the constituent events are held in some sort of continuity of aim or intention, whether this is consciously or unconsciously entertained. Of course, the potentiality for each given occasion may not be vividly realized. When things are going rightly, toward actualizing their potentiality, the achievement is not independent of other occasions but in real dependence upon them. There is an interrelationship here that impels us to think organically. Human existence is a clear instance of this social process. Thus, we must say that each human life affects and influences others, as it is itself affected and influenced by them. We know that we cannot escape our social context; it is an inescapable fact for us humans, as for all else in the creation. Hence, we find fulfillment possible in just such social contacts with others of our kind. And this business of fulfillment implies goals toward which our existence points. Here once more is a human application of a general truth. With it we know also that we are able to decide, in some genuine freedom, for or against these goals, in that we can cut off one possibility by adopting another. Basically, the goal for each one of us is to become, in our belonging, as completely human as is possible for us. Alas, it is also possible for us to opt for nonactualization of the goal and thus to fall into sheer repetition of prior states or to rest content with the *status quo* and thereby fail to advance at all toward this completeness.

For us humans, as in the world as large, persuasion rather that coercion is effectual in bringing us to our potential self-realization. Often enough it may seem that force is more likely to bring this about; but probably all of us understand that robotlike obedience to imposed coercive measures is likely to produce violent negation, once we have become mature enough to recognize what is going on. It may be possible to force somebody to do this or that, but the result is usually a mechanical response and not a fully human one. A young man may coerce a girl to go through the motions of lovemaking; what he *cannot* do is to force the girl really to love him, responding to him as a free human person and participating gladly in the enterprise we call lovemaking.

Obviously there are limits to what is possible on the human (and on every other) level. There is a patterning or ordering of the world and of human existence that prescribes such limits. But for the effecting of the free movement toward fulfillment, lure or invitation or attraction is the chief means for drawing existence toward its possible goal. Many modern people in the West have lost sight of this fact, although in other cultures (as in Chinese Taoism) it has been well understood. For those who accept a religious interpretation of the world and human life, as we are doing in this book, there is another and related point. *God* is in the picture. Yet God is not only the supreme irrationality (as Whitehead said) in that deity cannot be "explained" in terms of ordinary concepts—although deity *can* be seen as what Whitehead styled the "chief exemplification" of the principles required to interpret things. God is also the all-inclusive reality who is initiative of creative advance and (for our present purpose this is equally significant) receptive of what that advance brings about. It is God who is the supreme lure or attraction and who invites (for the most part through creaturely or "secular" agencies) the response of the creatures as they move from their initial possibility toward their concrete actualization.

This tells us also that God is affected and influenced by what happens in the world and in human life. I have noted this on earlier pages; here it is only necessary to add that precisely this fact gives existence, and for us *a fortiori* human existence, its value or what Whitehead called its "importance." Human life is not "a tale told by an idiot, full of sound and fury, signifying nothing." On the contrary, as most of us know most of the time, there is a deeply felt sense of genuine value; this is what makes life worth living, as it is often said. So there is a dignity about the human enterprise. No man or woman is unimportant or pointless, however worthless he or she may appear to be. Thus, each of us, as a person, plays a part and has a place in the ongoing of creation—"we count" and what we do counts also.

We also, like every other bit of existence, have a certain real causative capacity. Our decisions, made in such genuine freedom as is ours, have their part in the wider and more pervasive creative advance. I have said that traditional theism usually considers God to be the only causative agent that has any great significance, everything else possessing what at best is a derivative and ultimately a "Pickwickian" causative role. That means that God has been seen as absolutely omnipotent or all-controlling, while creaturely agents have little if anything to do ultimately with what goes on. Furthermore, when God is thus conceived, God does not have a *real*, but only a logical, relationship with that creation; God is not affected by it in any important way. But if our argument in this book is correct, the real situation is very different. The creative advance depends in part on us, in our causative capacity. Not that we are all that matters and that there is no more-than-human agency at work in the cosmos; but rather, that the value of our existence is both an expression of, and an agency available for, what God is up to in the world. That world is still in the making; thus, we are co-workers *with* God, if we will allow this to be true, even as we may also be working *against* God when we reject our basic human potentiality and "do wrong."

Now, since persuasion at the human level is the clue to the wider and all-encompassing cosmic aim or purpose, we can affirm that precisely as and when the human agent responds by deciding for, not against, the lure of love, the invitation comes to us to become more and more genuinely instrumental to that love—although "instrumental" is not exactly right, since our own self-realization is integral to the picture. It is too bad that some zealous theologians have tried to argue that this self-realization has been made (by those who talk in fairly secular terms) a substitute for the fulfillment of the divine purpose. But the truth is that talk of such *self-realization* is simply another way of stating what a Process theist sees to be *God's* purpose for us. One sometimes suspects that those theologians are fearful of losing their distinctive role by surrendering to secular understanding, and as a consequence they set up an intolerable dualism or dichotomy. They are possessed of "faithless fears" because they are deeply afraid of what seem to them to be "worldly" values. At all costs they must retain their job!

When we humans decide against responding in love to the divine lure, known to us under so many incognitos, we are at the same time and by the same token, denying our own potentiality as human. On the other hand, when we respond *in* love *for* love, and with it for the establishment of the justice that love desires and enacts, we are on the way toward realizing our potential humanity and becoming more truly what we have it in us to become. We are also lending our service, be it great or small and under whatever circumstances are available to us, to the great cosmic thrust for good. That is, we are serving *God.* Our human happiness is found there, at a level much deeper than in a superficial "pleasant feeling."

In such a religious context we can grasp more adequately what it means to be a human person. Scientific research and discovery, like everything else that we have learned about ourselves and the world, only gives this a wider setting and helps in deepening our genuine humanity. Thanks to work done in psychology and physiology, for instance, we know about ourselves as body-mind organisms; hence, we can understand more adequately the "dynamics" of personality. To think of ourselves as "souls" who happen to "inhabit bodies" for a short time is to deny the concrete reality of human existence. Incidently, it is also to reject the biblical view, in which we are said to be made of the stuff of the earth, upon which God breathes to create "living entities"— not "living souls," as the Authorized or King James Bible inaccurately translates the Hebrew of the Genesis story. We are indeed possessed of "spirit," but in the Jewish context this is not some object or "thing" but rather is a way of indicating relationships, with an openness of humans to others and to God. And to speak of "God's Spirit" is to say that God, too, is open to relationships.

In our human situation or condition, we are greatly impeded in the move to self-realization (or in religious idiom, to fulfillment in God) by the accumulated wrong doings we have inherited thanks to the causal efficacy of the past upon the present. Traditionally this had been called Original Sin. That is an unfortunate and misleading phrase. But the fact of that condition is very real, however unhappy may be the words used to indicate it. Hence, we cannot be cheerfully and easily optimistic about progress; it is not identical with process. On the other hand, we need not be entirely pessimistic. Good *can* be chosen and the right *can* be done. We need realism here, with due recognition given to both sides of the human story. We are responsible for the consequences of our decisions, not least as they have their affect upon how things go forward. Herein lies our accountability, both for our own becoming and for what we do with and about our belonging. Both our dynamism and our sociality or participation have their results. In our intimate contacts and in our wider relationships, what we do brings about a better or a worse situation. To be human is to be "on the way," along with our brothers and sisters; yet this is not necessarily the "right way," nor is our society necessarily a "good society" at any given moment.

Since human existence is a direction taken, rather than a point at which we have already arrived, further movement (together with an awareness of our human identity) will depend largely upon how we respond both to the past and to the impact of the present upon us. The future is in the picture, too, since inevitably we "project ourselves" toward the goals we have made our own. We have to decide how best we may arrive at those goals if they are good ones and avoid them if they are bad ones. In this, each one of us has his or her own speciality, since nobody's past or present options or future aims are simply identical with those of others. In that speciality, once again, we are complex body-mind creatures. Not only that of which we are consciously aware or subconsciously accept but also what might well be called the "visceral" or deeply bodily inheritance go toward making us what we are and offering possibilities for what we may become.

At our best we take for ourselves the "subjective aim" of moving toward complete humanness. What begins as the "initial aim" given by God in our very existence can be adopted as our own aim, and toward its achievement we may strive. Yet we are not alone. Our fellow humans are there, too. Above all, *God* is there, with the lures that augment this striving—in religious language, God's grace is working toward us, in us, for us, and with us. Or better put, *God* is thus working, because "grace" is nothing other than God in action and not something added onto or used by the divine reality itself.

In all this, the distinctively human quality is seen in our awareness and self-awareness. Whatever may be true elsewhere in the cosmos, the appearance of human life marked the emergence (after a long course of evolutionary development) of a kind of created occasion that can and does know itself and others, certainly with an intensity unparalleled (so far as we can see) elsewhere in the creation. Hence, we humans are to some degree "rational," with a capacity for understanding, thought, and introspection, as well as for observation. Each of us is also possessed of a volitional drive or energizing ability. Above all, each of us has deep feeling-tones. This last has been forgotten in a good deal of traditional analysis of human life, and failure to see that we have those "feeling-tones" is bound to produce a sadly distorted idea of personality. The "aesthetic," in this profound sense, with its expression in appreciation, evaluation, enjoyment or displeasure, and the like, is as much a part of our human experience as the rational and volitional aspects. Children whose aesthetic capacity is damaged or denied suffer tragically from this deficiency. This is why a sound education should have a place for the aesthetic (in this profound sense) to help the young person move toward real maturity, and all of us need to see and express this side of our selfhood. Alas, many men and women live impoverished lives because their aesthetic capacity has not been given much attention and they have not been helped to grow in an appreciative grasp of the world, of themselves, and of others.

Above all, however, human existence (whatever may and must be said about other levels of existence in the cosmos) is characterized by the possibility of loving. I mean here the conscious or partly conscious sharing or giving-and-receiving that marks relationship as its best. Sometimes this can be highly charged; often it may be fairly low-key. Depth of loving is our best human possibility—even if now and again (as psychologists tell us) it is of the love-hate variety. In this respect our humanness is a microcosmic expression of the macroscopic or divine reality of Love-in-action. In religious talk we rightly speak about our moving toward "the image of God" who *is* such Love-in-act. To become created lovers *is* to realize our human potentiality at its best. Thus, to be open to love is also to be open to God. Each of us, in his or her specific fashion, is intended by God to become a lover—and thereby to belong in a great cosmic society of loving of which human loving is a reflection.

What has been said thus far presupposes the freedom about which I have spoken so frequently. Granted that we do not have unlimited choice, we do yet have some such ability. All the arguments for determinism cannot convince us that we lack this freedom. Indeed, the most hardened determinists prove, by the very vigor of their effort to convince others of their case, the exact opposite of what they are seeking to demonstrate. As Bishop Butler said, it is silly to let arguments get in the way of this experienced fact. We all act as if we were free; that action is itself proof enough of our own genuine freedom. *What* we choose may be for right or wrong, as we all know; but this is part of what makes our human existence highly problematical for us.

The tragic truth is that to decide rightly is not easy. For centuries, as we have observed, the human race has had to accept the consequences of decisions made by those who went before. These often worked against proper human self-realization. The human race as a whole is in the situation that Paul Tillich described by the words *estrangement* and *alienation*. There are at least four aspects here. Each of us is alienated to some degree from his or her own proper destiny in the divine intention. Each of us is estranged, to a greater or lesser degree, from our fellow humans. Each of us is alienated, again in varying degrees, from the world of nature, which is our habitation and from which humankind has emerged. And each of us is estranged in some serious sense from the cosmic Love that would have us find our proper fulfillment in the accomplishment of greater good in the world. Such alienation or estrangement brings about a sense of human frustration, sometimes felt very keenly but more often and with most of us in something like Thoreau's "quiet desperation," known at moments when we cannot sleep or when we are not happy about what we have been doing or thinking. In religious language this is our condition as sinners. In secular idiom, it is our failure rightly to move on in our becoming and belonging.

Such a situation does not imply that we are totally corrupt, with nothing good about us and with no possibility of a change by which we may once again respond rightly to the circumambient lures and begin moving in the truly fulfilling direction. To think of ourselves as totally corrupt would be far too pessimistic; it would not take account of the patent fact that there *is* much goodness in the world and in human experience as we know it. In recent years some influential theologians have revived that negative view and have talked like the older Calvinistic scholastics about humans as "lost souls." The wisdom of the race, however, both in its secular expression and in its religious teaching, has spoken otherwise. That wisdom has indeed acknowledged the problematical situation of men and women and has conceded honestly that "we are not able of ourselves to help ourselves," if this is taken to suggest that we can change "all on our own." Yet it has also testified to a residual goodness in the world and in human life, so that the situation is not hopeless.

In various ways wise men and women have shown their conviction, based on their own experience and observation, that the stuff of which humans are made is *good* stuff and that human potentiality remains a *good* potentiality. In traditional Christian teaching at its best, this is seen in the distinction that has been made between the "image of God," in which we are made or toward which we are intended to move, and the "likeness of God," which has been seriously damaged by us. To be sure, this distinction between "image" and "likeness" is based on a mistaken exegesis of the Genesis story. But Irenaeus of Lyons, who first made the point, may have been wrong in his exegesis but splendidly right in the point he was getting at when he made it.

Every area of human existence has certainly been affected by our human situation as well as by our own decisions and actions; yet this need not equal, and in the most characteristic Christian thought has never been thought to equal, a condition of "total depravity." Decision for the good is not impossible, even if it is extraordinarily difficult in many circumstances. In any event, the love of God, working in and with us as a lure toward the right, is never absent. Of course, we shall make mistakes and in that way contribute to the further implementation of a bad situation. On the other hand, we may so respond to the lure of God (often enough in what I have consistently called its secular expression) that we may be enabled to make some contribution, however small it may seem, to the ongoing process toward greater good. Thus, we can both acknowledge our failures and accept our responsibility, while we are prepared to "stand up and be counted" for what we have been and done. We must do this bravely, with honest readings to admit imperfection and failure. But the cosmic process itself sets limits to our capacity to wreck it; this is where the cosmic thrust or dynamic we call God may exercise a kind of control beyond the usual persuasive mode of its expression.

Christian faith has something to add here. It speaks about our "redemption" by God. That establishes the high relevance of Christianity to human living. It asserts that the divine Love, operative at every moment and in every part of the creation, is always available to the creatures. But even more than that, it asserts that the divine Love is prepared to accept us as we are and for what we may become, to forgive the wrongs we have done, and at the same time to employ our obviously imperfect human existence for better and fuller realization of good in the future. The theological term for this Christian assertion is "justification by grace through faith." It does not for a moment argue that evil *is* good. But it holds that even the worst decisions and actions of men and women, with the appalling results they have brought about, can somehow be used by God if what we do is offered to deity and, thus, can become the occasion for a deepening awareness of, and a better response to, Love's demands and Love's readiness to assist them in their human situation.

We humans are continually being challenged to decide as best we can, in the light of such knowledge as is available to us; to act upon those decisions; to be open to as many good possibilities as can be envisaged but not to hesitate to make necessary choices among them; and above all to trust confidently that God values both us and our contributions. So it is that the creative God is also the redeeming God. Humans may be "freed to love," as I like to put it, although of themselves alone they find it impossible to do that. In spite of our inadequacy, as well as our repeated defection, there is still hope for us.

I have been writing in what may seem to some to be a highly abstract fashion. I do not apologize for this; but I admit gladly that W.H. Auden put the point in much less abstract, indeed in a telling and moving, manner when he wrote the following lines:

> And to the good who know how wide the gulf, how deep,
> Between Ideal and Real, who being good have felt
> The final temptation to withdraw, sit down, and weep,
> We pray the power to take upon themselves the guilt,
> Of human action, though still as ready to confess
> The imperfection of what can and must be built,
> The wish and power to act, forgive, and bless.
> (in *Letters from Iceland*)

4

Personal Human Relationships

Human existence is the enterprise of becoming a created finite lover, in which each person belongs to society. The aim or goal is the increase of good among all the participants. But to put it in that way is to overlook the equally important fact that each of us has his or her own specificity or speciality; it is also to fail to notice that men and women desire most of all that there shall be *an* other—a person who can become, in the belonging that is a necessary factor, the "dearest and best." This need not exclude other less intimate relationships, for to love *an* other usually brings about a further readiness for and an openness to other contacts, less intensive but very real, with other persons who are not *the* chosen other. When such openness and readiness is absent, the relationship between the primary two can very well become jealous and possessive. And if this happens, what is seen is not really love but an expression of self-centeredness and often a hidden wish to control. Love is mutuality, not ownership, and one way it can be achieved is precisely through the wider kind of contacts and concerns.

Human loving in its personal aspect might be seen as the first of a series of concentric circles, whose point of departure (so to say) is the self in its personal identity. We should love ourselves and have self-esteem; there is nothing to be said for rejecting or negating this. Jesus is reported to have taught that we "should love our neighbor as ourselves," and that implies that each of us can have an entirely proper self-concern, which is very different from self-centeredness to the exclusion of others in our general belonging. Then, a second circle is the kind of relationship we have with our family or our immediate friends. A third circle is to be seen in our community or the neighborhood of which we are part. And beyond this, there is still another circle where we are concerned with our fellows in our country or nation (I shall call this, for convenience sake, the "city"), making us English or American or Russian or Chinese. Finally, there is the human race as a whole and the natural setting in which all of us exist. It will not be possible in these chapters to give attention to all of these circles. What we shall do is to speak first in this chapter of what I call "personal human relationships," while in the two following chapters our interest will be centered on "familial relationships" and broader "social relationships" (including neighborhood and the like, with reference also to the significance of the "city"). A final topic will be "the religious community"; this must be discussed because the orientation here adopted includes human existence together with, in, and under God, the primal cause and the final affect.

The reason for this last inclusion ought to be apparent. In and through all the circles, a response is being made, rightly or wrongly, for good or for ill, to the world at large and, beyond that, to the cosmic Love-in-act. Thus, we have to do with what the philosopher Josiah Royce used to call "world loyalty." Hence, there is always a genuine religious response, although this may not necessarily be made in a vividly conscious fashion. In the different religions of the world, however diverse these may be in their ideas of deity and of human fulfillment, or even in their substitution of some other devotion like Buddhist Nirvana, there is just such a "religious" response.

A rightly developing personality is related in differing ways and with differing intensity with the whole range of reality, and humans are becoming what they have in them to become in their response to this whole range, again with differing intensity and with various kinds of awareness. Incidently, it is worth our noting that the very word *response* has two meanings. One is precisely this "answering back" or response in the usual sense; another, which in common usage becomes "responsibility," is our human accountability for what we do (or fail to do) in making just such a response. About this more will be said later.

Here we need also to recall our earlier insistence on the body-mind complex, which is our human existence, with its rationality, volition, moral capacity, and (above all, perhaps) aesthetic aspect and with its ability to give and receive in love. To remember this is to bring to mind that we are speaking of a unity of selfhood. This needs to be taken seriously at every level but nowhere so much as in the circle of one-to-one relationships with *an* other. For we humans love with our body as well as with our mind or "soul," although this does not necessarily or always entail specifically genital contacts.

It will be useful to begin this chapter by giving due consideration to this broad fact about us and to see our human sexuality, in its deepest sense, as having much to do with how we respond. Each of us is a sexual creature like others in the animal kingdom, although our human sexuality is also different from that which we observe in that kingdom. There is a distinctive human kind of sexuality, both in the broader sense and also in the narrower genital sense.

In the animal realm, as a simple biological fact, the sexual drive, desire, and equipment are directed toward the reproduction of the race, with a high degree of excitation to promote this—and perhaps also with some trace of affection on the part of those who engage in sexual activity. At the specifically human level, however, the primary function of the sexual desire, drive, and equipment is not reproductive but conjunctive or unitive. Of course, this does not make procreation unimportant or merely incidental. With persons of differing gender, the possibility of conception is usually present. Where a morally responsible decision has been taken by the partners, this is likely to be a consequence of sexual intercourse, and it is obviously right and desirable.

Part of the distinctively human expression of pervasive sexuality is the bringing of children into the world, at least for those who are not celibate (where such contact does not occur) or homosexual (where procreation is not possible).

But it is also the case that the children are, or should be, desired by their parents and not accidentally conceived and also that those children should have care and wise training. This is why, in my conviction, contraception in the sense of "planned parenthood" is a moral duty. To reduce humans in their physical sexual activity to the level of the barnyard is surely wrong, and it is odd that those who ban contraception (save for the "rhythm" method) are, in fact, making just that reduction, certainly with good intentions, but thereby involving themselves in a strangely self-contradictory position. For in humans sexuality is the bodily and psychological basis for the possibility of shared love. This is plainly true for heterosexual persons; it is, I think, equally true for homosexual persons, about whom I shall have something more to say later in this chapter.

The meaning of human sexuality, then, is primarily relational. It is an essential component of human existence. Each of us is a sexual creature, as I have indicated; this is nothing to be ashamed of. It is integral to our nature as human and is part of our total human development in becoming and belonging. We are not with others simply "in our minds." We are with them in the concrete reality of our full humanness. Thus, human sexuality is a "doing," whether explicitly genital or not; it is not merely a "thinking" matter. In all our relationships with others, our sexuality is involved, although we are not consciously aware of this all the time. Even friendship between two persons, without such explicit acts, has its sexual component, and it should be acknowledged honestly. Failure to recognize this has led to much that is warped and twisted in human life. The "spinster" type (more often found among men than among women, I believe), the hypercritical person who is frequently also hypocritical, the nasty-mindedness often seen in persons who seem to be afraid of or to dislike anything remotely sexual, are not happy examples. If I really love another, I love that other with my whole self, not just with a selected portion of that self—and in that wholeness the sexual component is unquestionably present.

To accept this is very important, especially in Anglo-Saxon lands where it has been thought for a long time that

44

some human relationships can be totally platonic, spiritual, mental, nonphysical. This has led many people to fear such contacts as are found in Latin countries, where touching, kissing, embracing, and the like are taken for granted. We may conclude that in those countries there is a much healthier, because a more total, awareness of how humans function. Perhaps their acceptance of such contacts helps to explain why, as experts have told us, there are fewer serious emotional disturbances of a neurotic or psychotic kind than in our own lands. The sad truth is that many of us entertain, although not always consciously, a Manichean attitude toward the body, as part of a similar negative attitude toward the material world. We are altogether *too* "spiritual," rejecting or minimizing our embodiedness, which we tend to think to be somehow unfortunate or sometimes even "dirty."

That distaste or fear can be, in itself, a dangerous and damaging matter. What is even worse, it can lead to repressions that turn humans into suspicious and (as I have said) hypercritical or hypocritical creatures whose presence makes others uncomfortable and whose own inner lives can become frustrated and miserable. My point here is simply that the pervasive reality of sexuality is given in our human experience and is an entirely good thing. C.S. Lewis once put this neatly, "God must like sex, he *made* it." To accept this fact gladly, even joyously, is part of healthy human living. And as Lewis indicated in that brief remark, it is part of our gratitude to God to see that such sexuality is one of God's good gifts that we are to use responsibly. That responsibility requires a certain human "control," as we shall argue in the sequel—not control as servile obedience to imposed regulations set by society or even by God, but as useful guidelines to the best ways in which to express this inescapable part of our human existence.

One way of getting at the point is by considering the celibate man or woman whose specific vocation is not to act genitally but to redirect the sexual drive, desire, and equipment for other ends that are taken as good for that particular person. It may seem surprising to introduce such people at this place, but it is a great mistake to assume that monks and nuns in Catholic circles, or the members of the similar Taizé community among Protestants, have *killed* their sexuality. Doubtless, in the past many sought to do just that, but nowadays few if any monks or nuns would be willing to say that he or she has done this or wishes to do this. Sometimes, to be sure, men and women in an earlier age became celibate because of their fear of sexuality or because there was no other available place for them in society. They were expected in such instances "to put their sexuality to death," as the saying went. Not today, however. I think here of an Oxford monk who indignantly denied that he had done any such thing; what he had done, he said, was to seek a rechannelling of his sexual nature so that instead of having genital contacts he could express this human drive by serving others, by teaching, and by prayer. I think also of a nun whom I once knew well. In her presence one felt that one was with a person who used her inescapable sexuality to help other persons in a lovely, attractive, and entirely nongenital way.

There is a distinction, then, but not a separation, to be made between the deep, pervasive sexuality that is integral to our human nature, on the one hand, and the various ways (some genital, some in self-giving without genital contact) of expression of that sexuality, on the other.

I have mentioned homosexuality, and a few words should be said about that sort of sexual expression, to which (we have been informed) perhaps 10 percent of the human family are oriented. In the past, people who were homosexually inclined, and especially those who were active in that respect, were regarded as sinful, corrupt, or criminal. Today they are seen by understanding people to be different but not deviant. They are the way they are through no choice of their own. What they should be given is assistance, when this is wanted, to live their lives happily and well, following their own orientation without condemnation or contempt. Happily, today those who are not blinded by uncriticized religious prejudice (including misuse of certain biblical passages) or conventional ideas of proper sexual behavior (as if morals were a matter of counting noses or following some social pattern without question) are ready to accept the fact of the homosexual orientation, and many religious groups are now prepared to adopt this positive attitude.

But if for homosexual people intimate relationships are more readily found with someone of their own gender, it is obviously true that the great majority of men and women find their fulfillment with people of the other gender. For most of these, the way for this expression is through the estate of marriage or some similar sharing of life together. This will include familial life, to which we turn in the next chapter. Here our concern is simply with the intimate relationship with *an* other, without necessarily involving such family life, the care of children, and whatever else has become part of the common manifestation of personal relationship. Certainly a one-to-one relationship deepens and develops human existence. At the same time, however, there is a possible distortion in that kind of belonging, which then produces unlovely results. In that case, there can be tragic twistings, jealousy, possessiveness, and other damaging consequences. I shall now say something about some aspects of this distortion, all of them of course related to the basic sexuality of humankind.

Before I do that, however, there is another point that should be made. I suppose some might think that the result of such a discussion as this would be to set up, as a sort of ideal, what is nowadays called "the well-adjusted person." I can only say, "God forbid!" if that is taken to mean the type often commended by certain followers of the "mental health" school, with no idiosyncrasies, no distinctive qualities, no particular marks of speciality. People like that are so well-adjusted to the expectations of conventional society that they become boring and dull. Anybody who is perfectly adjusted to contemporary conventional society is really very badly adjusted to the basic reality of things in the cosmos! Hence, far from urging any such model, I should urge that each person, in his or her specificity, is intended to become what *he* or *she* has the potential for becoming—and that will mean great variety, many differing types of fulfillment and self-realization, each with its value and importance. The common principle here is only that each human should be moving toward actualization, with others, in and under the divine Love—a Love, one may be sure, that prefers variety, novelty, and even oddity (if I may say so!) to the sheer uniformity that is to be found in products of a machine.

With this clear, let us now proceed to speak of the five aspects of human defection that seem to be the most serious manifestations of distortion in relationship. First of all, such a relationship can be consciously or unconsciously centered upon oneself, without due regard for the other person in it. Here there is a denial of the belonging side of human experience. One person may be so centered on himself or herself that the two cannot really share life, excepting in the most superficial fashion. Second, there can be the treatment of the other as if he or she were a thing, not a person. To be a person is to be a particular routing of experiences toward goals that satisfy latent potentialities special to each of us. But it is tragically possible to neglect or overlook this and to act with and toward another as if the other's importance lay simply in providing a means toward one's own satisfaction. Third, there can be cruel or hateful manifestations, either directly or in subtle psychological fashion; in either case, this is damaging to self-esteem in the other and turns that other into an object to be compelled and coerced. Fourth, in denial of such self-esteem or in disregarding it there can be the assumption of a wrong kind of responsibility, with a callous disregard of deepest opportunities for sharing life. As a young woman once said to me, "When somebody tells me that he will be responsible for me, I feel that he's denying that I'm a real person and looks upon me as merely instrumental to his own desires!"—this is nothing less than a subtle variety of rape. Fifth, there can be such a focus upon one particular aspect of the relationship (in specifically sexual matters, this may be an interest only in the physical side) that the total human personality is not taken into account, in all its richness and promise. In effect, each of these is basically a failure in genuine loving, as we shall see at the end of this chapter.

If we now turn to the first, or to wrong self-centeredness, it is obvious that we have here a denial of genuine reciprocity or mutuality. It is focused on what can be "got" from the other. Here there may *seem* to be some sort of giving, but it is a giving that is interested only in "the main chance" or in what the other may be persuaded to do or be. There may be some sort of response to the other, but this can be grudging and thoughtless, because it is only a way of using the other to secure what is wanted for the self. Of course, I am not here condemning the self-assertion that is proper if each of us is to have personal integrity and identity. Nobody need make himself or herself a doormat for others to trample under foot. That would be an inverted form of the pride that goes with total self-concern. But anybody who is arrogant, contemptuous of others, and thus wholly centered in self can never enter into deeply fruitful relationships. That sort of person is a fraud. The becoming that is so essential can only be had when the other's becoming is recognized and valued for itself and not simply as adjectival to self.

A second and related sort of distortion is the depersonalization of the relationship. The other may be treated as something to be used, not as one who is accepted in his or her own becoming. This can happen in subtle ways, not always obvious to an observer. The truth is that genuine love always personalizes; in doing so it respects and values the personal integrity and identity of the other. In any sort of human contact, it is possible to be moving in this direction. Casual contacts with others, even on such limited occasions as dealing with those who serve one in a shop, can do that. They can have the possibility, however slight, of personalization, or alternatively someone can regard the other as a thing that is there only for her or his own benefit. In that latter case the other is reduced to a mere object—for instance, in one's casual contact with a shop assistant, where there could be no close relationship but where at best there might be friendliness and courtesy, the other could just as well be a vending machine. In more intimate relationships with *the* other, something of this sort can also happen. One *uses* the other for one's own pleasure or satisfaction. And genuine love can never do that.

A third aspect of distortion is cruelty or actual damage

to the partner. This sadistic attitude and pattern of behavior is plainly seen in certain kinds of physical sexuality. But it is also present in carelessness and indifference that are not explicitly sexual in the genital sense. In civilized society and among civilized persons, this sadism may be somewhat tempered, yet in person-to-person relationships it can be dreadfully apparent. The cutting comment, the unkind phrase, or the inconsiderate act may inflict frightful pain. Often this is not actually intended, but its avoidance demands from each one attention to the other and to the other's feelings. It is also to be remembered that the person who acts sadistically is himself or herself a victim, quite as much, if less obviously, as is the actual object of the word or act. Fullness of human self-realization is denied to both, and this contradicts the love that is intended or desired.

A fourth aspect of distortion has to do with responsibility. I have noted that in our being thus responsible we should never fail to entertain a genuine esteem for the other. That other is to be accepted in and for himself or herself and never left to assume that her or his value is simply in being "available." Above all, the other cannot be made to feel that he or she is not worth very much. In giving help to the other in some problem or difficulty, the giving can be done in a way that puts the recipient at a disadvantage so that he or she is made to feel less of a person. But this need not be so; it is always possible to assist without condescension and without allowing the recipient to sense, somehow or other, that the donor is *deigning* to act kindly and helpfully.

Finally, there is the danger of denying proper proportion or patterning, in such a way that one particular element or aspect of the relationship is made so central that its wholeness or totality is denied or at least called into question. In the Middle Ages, this lack of proportion or patterning was known as *inordination.* For example, physical relations are good in themselves, as expressions of genuine love and mutuality; when they are all that matters in the relationship, they become patently *inordinate* and no longer can symbolize and augment mutuality or the sharing of total life. Similarly, a certain shared interest may originally draw people together, but if that is all they have in common, then wholeness is denied or minimized. Wider sharing provides a healthy setting for particular shared interests. Love is concerned to establish just that wider sharing.

In all these kinds of possible distortion, then, there is a rejection of real loving, although often, perhaps usually, this is not intended. Love moves toward a fulfillment in which each partner genuinely shares. Its contradiction can be found in each of the concentric circles and perhaps nowhere so obviously as in person-to-person relationships. Needless to say, this is not a matter of sentimentality; it is not mere emotionalism; it is not easy toleration. On the contrary, it can be adamant, difficult, demanding; yet it is always gracious, generous, and helpful. In our intimate one-to-one relations, with *an* other, there is much more intense caring; but even in ordinary day-to-day contacts there can be something of that same quality.

For the majority of members of the human race, as I have urged, this most intimate relationship is found in the estate of marriage, although in close friendships and in homosexual orientation it can also be present. Here I wish to speak very briefly about the way in which marriage may provide an occasion for distortion and damage. Even in the best of human institutions, of which marriage can serve as a supreme example, there can be damage when somehow the intention to share life fully is absent. Here is a one-to-one relationship *par excellence.* But it is not to be achieved without effort, although it is at its best when there is also real spontaneity in the expression of love together. And it may break down. Its preservation requires effort, and it is worth the trouble it takes to ensure its continuance. On the other hand, when there is an utter collapse of mutuality, it is surely better to recognize the fact and to separate. To paraphrase a saying of Jesus, "Marriage was made for man, not man for marriage." This enormously valuable and valued estate is not a straitjacket nor is it a Procrustean bed in which human capacities and talents are to be lopped off to accommodate men and women to an imposed condition of miserable union. If that is recognized, we must also admit that divorce may be the right thing under such tragic circumstances.

What it comes down to, then, is our understanding that human existence, in its becoming and in its belonging, is a direction for creative advance. By their very nature, humans are intended to be moving toward fulfillment in love, in mutuality and sharing, so that those who participate in any relationship, and above all in the intimate one that can be enjoyed with *an* other, may be given the opportunity to find satisfaction and realization of potentiality in and with this other and with others. Such a direction of life is open to newness, with a greater future sharing, while in the present moment there is delight and happiness. What is more, such love can overflow; of this possibility, the child or children in a marriage stand as a symbol. The two can create with their offspring a little cell of creative loving.

The human enterprise is a great adventure, as we move from the relatively settled world of our past, through decisions and actions in the present, toward the unexplored but alluring world of the future. This forward movement gives zest to life, as Whitehead rightly saw and said. In no area is this adventure so promising as in the one-to-one, person-to-person, relationships where two human lives are glad to share and work together, for the best good of each and with love as the motivation and resource as well as the result of that sharing.

I conclude with one final point. Such genuine love is marked by a joy that rises above duty; it can be "fun." Why is this? The answer surely is that right functioning is always characterized by a deep sense of well-being. We know this about our bodies. When they are functioning rightly there is a basic contentment. So also for the whole range of our existence. When we are moving in the direction proper to us as humans we enjoy a feeling of satisfaction. This does not imply unimaginative, stolid, or dully repetitive existence. On the contrary, there may be and there should be something of a "divine discontent" in all human life, since none of us is fully and entirely what we have in us to become. There will be a striving toward as well as a desire for more and better things. At the same time there can be a wonderful happiness and a deep sense of joy in our relationship one with *an* other.

5

Familial Relationships

The first of the concentric circles beyond the self is that which has to do with *an* other, the person with whom we are in most intimate relationship. The second circle, to which we turn in this chapter, is what I have here called "familial"—that is to say, with our family or in similar groupings. By the family I do not mean only what nowadays sociologists call "the nuclear family"—husband, wife, and children. What we shall be considering is the relatively close-knit unit or group, composed of a few people—normatively, of course, a family in the ordinary sense but also other possible associations that involve the presence of a person with several others, so that there can be an expression of belonging, with mutual love and concern, sympathy, and understanding, and hence the opportunity and occasion for enrichment and growth in each of the participants. Perhaps one may think here of communes or of very close friends with whom one finds real companionship.

We have seen, in the intimate relations of person-to-person, negative possibilities that can seriously damage if not destroy the relationship. Here, as we turn to larger groupings, we may profit by looking at the positive side. When we do this, we shall have a useful indication of the elements that constitute a healthy and mature existence as this may be shared in exactly such familiar situations or in those that resemble them.

The negatives have been self-centeredness, deper- sonalization, cruelty, carelessness or irresponsibility, and disproportionate emphasis upon one single aspect of the relationship—and with these a joylessness in the linking of one with *an* other. The positives, therefore, will be an awareness of others and a sharing of life with them, an augmenting of personal identity and integrity, an upbuilding in healing and caring, concern for the others that will not permit cruelty or carelessness, and a stress upon the wholeness of each in the grouping—and with all these, a joy in being together which makes the common life delightful and aesthetically fulfilling or harmonious. As we went through the negatives, so here we shall go through the positives. For the positives respond to, and at the same time manifest, human needs and their satisfaction. Just as in one-to-one relationships the negatives damage and may destroy, so the positives (now applied to familial groupings) will produce right ways of becoming and, hence, promote sound and healthy development. In such groupings, seen positively, there is the opportunity for a genuine flowering of human potentiality. Perhaps this is why the family and suchlike groupings are commonly regarded as among the most rewarding of all modes of human community.

In our relationships with one other person, but also in the larger familial relations we are now considering, what is being sought and from time to time achieved is genuine mutuality. It is in fact belonging in a very real sense, where one knows others and enjoys being with them, yet with due regard for their integrity and for their personal identity. They are not thought to be "individuals" in isolation from others; their belonging seems instinctively to entail a desire to share in common concerns and interests. The loner, who has no such urge, is not very typical of most of the human race. He or she may best be seen, perhaps, as someone whose natural human wish for sharing has somehow been warped or stunted, maybe in early childhood or at a later stage where there has been a sense of rejection or disregard. Normally and typically, every man and woman wants and seeks for companionship of some sort, not only with those who are closest but with others as well.

I have already urged that it is a mistake to think that humans are by nature totally self-centered. The error arises from a wrong interpretation of the obvious fact that every-body wants to be a self, to have a sense of the value of his or her selfhood, and to realize, so far as may be, the potentialities given in that selfhood. Thus, self-awareness and even a degree of self-concern are both necessary for each of us and also a condition for the sharing that each seeks. Without such specific identity and the related integrity of self there would be nothing to share; we should all of us be lost in a repetition of the same thing over and over again. There would be a dull and uninviting uniformity that would fail to seek, find, and value the variety and difference that makes human existence both delightful or enjoyable and also painful. The union of persons, both in the more intimate sense and in the wider sense of degrees of sociality, requires that there be distinct persons, each marked by his or her own speciality, with whom association may be found. Of the pain that this necessarily entails we shall speak later; here let it be said that it is erroneous to assume, as have some careless theologians and sociologists among others, that human wrong is located in self-concern. The truth is that everybody needs to be aware that he or she counts in the total human picture. Wrong enters the picture only at the point where this entirely natural and necessary self-concern becomes the controlling interest, so that others are given no place in thought and practice. That is the contradiction of mutuality and is the kind of belonging in which other persons are taken to be only adjectival to one's own existence.

It is easily seen that familial groupings of the kind we are now discussing are made possible only through this wish for mutuality. Common enterprises, shared concerns, pursuit of agreed upon goals, and the like provide for us the means through which giving-and-receiving may be attained. But they should not become exaggerated or obsessive, so that there is nothing else in the relationship. A husband and a wife have their shared concern for their children, if they have any; they are concerned also about the house in which they live and about whatever initial interests may have drawn them together in the first place. In participation one with the other they find a genuine fulfillment of selfhood, and society at large is enriched by this achievement. A central devotion to what we may style "the common good" is part of the sense. When Rollo May writes in his book *Paulus* (p. 113) about his friend and teacher Paul Tillich, he speaks about Tillich's relationships with others by saying, "His love for us was relentless in his . . . insistence on our best. It was a magnificent grace to us that he would not let us escape from becoming what we truly are." Here we see both a deep appreciation of each for herself or himself and a readiness to demand this from those with whom one is associated. At the same time, in the devotion to a common good—in this case, to the particular subject in which both have an interest—there is a fine instance of healthy and enriching ways of promoting for each the fullest realization of selfhood that is possible. Each of us, in becoming, needs exactly some such awareness of belonging with others in the total human enterprise.

Tied in with this is our second point. Familial life when at its best is so ordered that the personal quality of others is augmented; they cannot be treated as if they were merely objects or things to be used by one person simply to promote that person's own development. This is an implication of genuine love. Such love cannot conceivably wish to "thingify" or depersonalize; when we see depersonalizing taking place, we can be sure that instead of love we have only a sentimental substitute or what amounts to a mere pretension (romantic or tolerant) for true concern. Words are easy to speak, but what is important in relationships is acts done, rather than chatter, and done in a manner that assists growth in others.

If this is true, then it is obvious that a familial grouping cannot be marked by cruelty, whether this is of a plainly physical sort or the more subtle (but more harmful) kind that likes to make others feel uncomfortable or unwanted or unnecessary. Love forbids such cruelty. Love is always for healing and never for hurting. In intimate relationships this sadism can be terrible in its effects; so also in familial groupings it can be frightening in the way in which it damages integrity and leads to a deterioration of character not only in the victim but also in the one who inflicts the harm. On the other hand, concern for others expressed in helpful and upbuilding action results in the best growth of all who are in the group—including, once again, the person who shows this concern.

Such dedication to the good of others does not imply a lack of firmness nor does it acquiesce readily in less than the best. The quotation from Rollo May about his friend and teacher Paul Tillich shows that one of the ways in which genuine caring is manifested is precisely in the insistence that others shall "become what they truly are," to use May's own phrase. In other words, they are assisted in realizing their potentialities and are (so to say) incited to move in that direction. Nothing can be worse than indifference in this matter; such unconcern has the effect of cruelty, even if often quite unconsciously, by negating the other. There is an old saying that speaks about "being cruel to be kind." That is an unhappy way of putting it, for cruelty is never right. But it probably is intended to point to what I have called firmness, and what others have styled "adamant demand," in the expectation of, as well as in an insistence upon, the best from others. This shows love in a way much deeper than the *laissez-faire* attitude that is easy to adopt but often enough is only a demonstration that there is no real caring at all.

Most of us can testify to the sense of hurt we have felt when someone with whom we thought we were in close rapport in some group of friends—or in family life in the narrower sense—demonstrates by act that he or she does not *really* very much care for us. Many a family or group of close friends can bear witness to the damage done when one of its members is like that or when the whole group shows carelessness. The consequence is a sense of discouragement, for it implies disregard or dismissal from consideration. This may not be cruelty in either the physical or psychological sense, narrowly interpreted, but certainly it *is* cruelty in that it is a failure to recognize and respond to the personal quality of each member. What Coleridge used to call "personeity" is integral to the human self; it must be respected. When it *is* respected, there can be a remarkable flowering of hitherto unsuspected possibility. Like a rose that opens its petals when the sun shines upon it, this or that person may open up in a remarkable manner.

There is no place where one or the other of these—augmenting or diminishing—may be more effectual than in familial groups.

Does each care for all? That is the basic question here, and it is related immediately to the responsibility about which I have spoken. This responsibility includes the two factors of readiness to respond to others who are associated with us and our accountability in respect to those others. The latter can be possible only when the former is present. The one who can take seriously his or her accountability for others is the one who first of all has "answered back" to the reality of those others. In groupings like the family, the importance of this can readily be seen; if I do not respond to my husband or wife or children, in that profound sense, I am all too likely to be careless about responsibility for them and to them. But when there is on my part an openness and a genuine responsiveness, I find myself seriously involved and know that in however small a degree I am accountable for them and to them. There is a deepening of mutuality and a growing-together in the relationship that is rewarding and joyous.

This carries with it a concern for what I have styled the "self-esteem" of others. That means that I cannot let them think that they have no value in themselves; I cannot "take care of them" as if they were worthless or incompetent or helpless. The integral selfhood of the others, each with his or her self-esteem, demands that I acknowledge them for themselves, with the capacity to make their decisions and "do their own thing." No other, however closely knit with me in some grouping, is an extension of myself; to think that way, above all to act as if that were the case, is destructive of the giving-and-receiving that can characterize human belonging when it is functioning at its best.

This is why awareness of and sensitivity to mutuality or sharing must be part of familial existence. This closeness, however, needs to be put in the context of other and wider contacts. Without that context, there is the danger that the family and its like will become so focused on itself, so inward-looking, that it becomes a cell of unhealthy life, not of healthy and developing life. Sociologists and anthropologists have spoken of the way in which the nuclear family—the small group of three or four persons—can be vicious because it *may* (not *must*) become centered on its own existence and, hence, entirely inward-looking—like a pond with no outlet. The small group is especially open to danger here. A married couple with one or two children can spend all their time and effort on themselves. They can lose sight of the larger community, save insofar as they are anxious to keep up appearances. They can try to make their neighbors and acquaintances think that they are sufficient unto themselves and, hence, reject advances from or toward others round about. The final result can be disastrous.

What Sir Edmund Leach in his Reith lectures a few years ago called "the dirty little secrets" of the group—by which he meant not sexual doings of one sort or another but the group's financial position, its petty maneuvers to maintain a place in society, its *secret* and "shameful" (as it sees it) dependence on hire-purchase plans or installment buying—may become so dominant that all its time and effort will be given to such worries. In the long run there is then a failure, since it is not possible for any group to be sufficient unto itself. We all need the give-and-take of our societal existence. And for what it is worth, it is useful to point out that what is here true for the familial relationships is also, and sometimes horribly, true in respect to neighborhoods, or cities, and nations. Ours is indeed a belonging world, and we can live well and happily only on such terms as are appropriate to such a world.

The analogue, in familial groups, to the disproportionate or "inordinate" emphasis on genital sexuality in one-to-one relationships is to be found in a total centering upon the particular associations of the group. Just as the physical union of two persons becomes rich and rewarding, and not only gratifying in a physical and emotional sense, when it is expressive of a wide sharing of life together, so also a family that is totally centered in itself, without concern for those around it and for the broader matters they represent, is likely to lose a great deal, while with such an awareness and wider sharing it is likely to be rich and rewarding. Total group-centering can be morbid and sick and even self-destructive. On the other hand, openness to others and delight in their presence and activity can give color and vitality to the group's own existence. A family—say, a couple with children—needs that context. From such contacts with the "outside world" opportunity is given for surprise, contrast, challenge, and joy. Thus, the family is delivered from what somebody has well called "the abyss of self-centered isolation."

I have spoken of joy, and this brings us to the last of the positive directives or guidelines for healthy and happy familial life. A group that does not experience such joy in belonging together is hardly likely to survive for very long, save by a superficial bonding of those who really have nothing in common. The members exist together, to be sure, but they find no delight or satisfaction in that association. But this joy is not to be had for nothing. This is why entrance upon familial life of any sort requires care in the selection of partner or partners, along with a willingness to spend oneself for the familial group being established.

In that selection, several factors play their part, such as common interests, but also a sufficient difference is needed so that life does not become monotonous. What is wanted is contrast but not conflict. A beautiful painting has no mere repetition of color and line but presents sufficient contrast to give variety and charm without setting up an ugly conflict among these colors and lines. This is even more obvious in music, where there must not be discordant opposition of theme and mood and style but a harmonization of these in a grand totality of sound. In a familial group something of this sort of pattern should also be present. Harmony is the precondition for the deepening of life together, with the joy this can bring. And as the years go by, each person in the group comes to understand the differences, to accept them, and to delight in them.

Thus, a family needs the positives that I have been presenting; it needs also to avoid, so far as possible, the negatives that are their opposite. But it is unlikely that any familial group is likely to achieve perfection in this or any other respect. Certainly genuine effort can help. But human life together, like the life of each one of us, is a becoming, not a static thing; it is a direction taken, a routing of experiences, toward a goal that is valued as important. Judgment at any point along the line should always be in terms of that direction or routing—this is true for a group as for a person. Specific momentary acts or thoughts or words have their significance in that they indicate whether or not the direction or routing is for the best ends. Failure to understand this and to come to terms with it will produce dissatisfaction and even pessimistic rejection of good already known. Or it may produce a kind of easy satisfaction with the *status quo*, acceptance of the partial good as if it were the fully realized one, or dismissal of the final goal through concentration on this or that specific problem.

I have said that the nuclear family is a fact of our own day. It is often defended as being the way things have always been, to such an extent that it is given an almost idolatrous devotion, not least in ethical and religious discussions. As a matter of fact, however, it is of fairly recent origin. In older times, as social historians have shown, the extended family was the normal arrangement, and it still continues to be normal in many parts of the world, even if in Western countries this is not always recognized. Such an extended family included in its membership relatives and other near members of the clan or sect or group. There would be grandparents, uncles, aunts, cousins, children, and, of course, the parents of the contemporary group or those who otherwise were in a position of leadership. The numbers and the kinds of membership varied, to be sure, from culture to culture, place to place, and time to time. But the grouping would cross generations and would bring together old and young, immediate and somewhat more remote family connections and siblings, and others, too—all of these might live in one place or sufficiently close so that a common life was possible. Even so recently as the days before the First World War, as some of the older of us can remember, it was quite normal for one or more grandparents, perhaps an aunt or an uncle or both, sometimes cousins of first-degree, and even others somewhat related, to share a house together or to be readily accessible in times of trouble or in moments of familial celebration. They would give help where this was needed; they would be consulted about problems; they would participate in family activities; and often they would have their part in family decision making.

Obviously, all this is not very frequent today, and in many parts of our Western world it has disappeared altogether. The familial group is smaller, not only because family planning has become a matter of ordinary practice but also because economic and social conditions have made large households almost impossible to maintain. Older people are likely to be cared for in special homes or communities for the aged and for those who have retired from active work. Sometimes, of course, the elderly prefer to be on their own. But even if they do not (and many do not) wish this, social pressures are sufficient to make them feel that it will be better for them not to burden others by their presence and demands.

One of the problems this situation has brought about is precisely the possibility of a far too ingrown and self-retarding attitude. The family is closed in upon itself and lacks genuine openness to others, especially those who by reason of consanguinity or similar status might provide fresh opportunities for enrichment and growth, with more challenges for new kinds of response and with awareness of the diversity of human existence. The end result may be a refusal to admit others at all; anybody who "butts in" will certainly be rejected. This need not happen; but it does indeed happen far too frequently. Doubtless we all know familial groups where this introversion is found.

Probably one of the main causes for the increasingly large numbers of divorces or separations in the usual family group is simply that husband or wife become bored or "fed up" with the narrowness and restrictions they meet. They then try to find something or someone new and interesting. Children can suffer badly in these circumstances, although they are better off when there is a real break if the parents are so bored with one another or even so dislike one another that the children's existence is made miserable. People often say that they will "stick together" because the children otherwise will have no "real home." Of course, the fact is that in such a situation these children do not have a "real home" in any serious sense. All they have is a place in which they can sleep and eat.

Familial life is not ideal or perfect most of the time. It can only have value if and as its members decide to work at it, not in a painfully severe fashion but with genuine willingness to do what they can to promote and augment the relationship, with due recognition of likely failures and with a readiness to accept these when they happen. But to do this requires forgiveness. That is to say, each must make allowances for the defects of others quite as much as being aware of his or her own defects. All must seek the good of each. To forgive is never easy; niether is acceptance of forgiveness. Yet without the spirit of forgiveness nobody can hope to share life with others. This is not the same as advocating cheap toleration or easy acceptance. True forgiveness demands a concern and care for others, a sincere readiness to cooperate with them so that their best may be achieved, and a faithful expectation that each can grow toward that best. Here, of course, the religious awareness of divine forgiveness provides the clue to what human forgiveness must be. And it requires always a not easily acquired willingness to take risks.

With forgiveness goes forbearance. Here is a situation in which "letting be," to use a phrase from Martin Heidegger with which John Macquarrie has made us familiar, is so important. Just as God's continuing creative activity does not directly "make" things but rather allows, encourages, and assists them to "make themselves," so in the familial group we can allow others to "make themselves," with all the difficulties this may seem to include. I believe that this principle runs through the whole cosmos, but its necessity is very plain for the familial relationship. Assumption of control by any one member of the group can have as a consequence the denial to others of the proper exercise of their capacity for free decision. When something like this happens, we no longer have a genuine *family* unit; instead, we have lord and servants, master and slaves, tyrant and submissive subjects. It becomes even worse when the servants, slaves, or subjects come to feel and to act as if this is the way things must be; then they have given up their human dignity and have denied the human potentiality that is properly theirs.

Probably most of us have known familial groups in which one of the parents assumes just such a position of total domination. If there are children, they will revolt. The parent will be greatly disturbed by this revolt, whether it is subtly expressed or when it is implemented in the child or children actually "leaving home" or manifesting outright and open rebellion. But the person or persons who are subjected to domination have not really had a "home." They have felt that they are in a prison, and they become (sometimes violently) antagonistic to the parent who, doubtless with good intentions, has denied them the freedom so essential to becoming truly human. It is tragic to see how frequently the one who dominates does this with "good intentions"; it reminds one of Pascal's saying that people "never sin so seriously as when they do it with good intentions."

I have said that in this chapter I am using the word *family* to include not only what is usually meant by that word but also other types or varieties of close relationship with more than *an* other. One of these, about which there is not time to speak in detail, is the "commune," a mode of grouping that in some parts of the Western world has become increasingly popular. Observers have predicted that this sort of social grouping will be the successor to the nuclear family. One may doubt that this will happen; yet certainly a commune can often come close to the old extended family, even if the reason for its existence is different. The fact remains that a considerable number of young people are now finding genuine fulfillment in life together in this new fashion.

But maybe it is not so new, after all. One thinks of monasteries and convents and similar small communities that have existed in the past and that exist even today. In those communities there are "rules," like the famous one devised by St. Benedict and still in force in the religious order he founded. This rule allows for considerable diversity yet establishes a remarkable unity among those who accept it. The trouble with such rules, however, is that they may be taken as absolute, without regard for the changes needed in adapting them to a new age. No rule can be final and complete; plainly enough, as the poet wrote, "new occasions teach new duties," while "time makes ancient good uncouth." Fortunately, this is realized today, and most of the followers of the "religious life" in convents and monasteries and similar communities have labored in recent years for a considerable relaxation, but without giving up their general agreement on basic principles. To a large degree, freedom is granted to the members, but they are still bound together by glad acceptance of the common life, and they use the rule as a guideline rather than as an arbitrarily imposed dictate.

A family grouping of any sort should be a cell of healthy and joyous caring, where warmth is felt and where love is experienced. Such groupings make possible remarkable development; they are enormously helpful to men and women in their becoming. And when we move from the intimate one-to-one relationship, through the sort or relationships with which in this chapter we have been concerned, to an even wider range (the third of my concentric circles) of human belonging in the broad social development of the human race, we shall find that many of the same principles hold good. Of the religious community, to which we shall later also give attention, this is obviously true. And the reason for this continuity is, I believe, that the very grain of the universe runs that way. In other words, these principles are in accordance with the divine activity in the creation.

6

Social Relationships

We have looked at one-to-one relationships with *an* other and at familial groupings of men and women. Thus, our discussion has included the first two of the concentric circles about which I have spoken. Now we turn to what I am calling the "social" circle. By this I mean the larger community that is part of our human existence and of which we ourselves are necessarily a part by virtue of our belonging in the city. I am using here the word *city* because Aristotle, the great Greek philosopher, spoke about it in what might be styled the second part of his treatment of ethics. The first part of his discussion in *The Nichomachean Ethics* has to do with what here we are calling more personal relationships. The second part is known to us as *The Politics*, and it must be remembered that for Aristotle, as for any Greek of his time, "politics" had to do with much more than the subject we nowadays indicate when we use this term. For a Greek life had its setting in one or other of the small city-states found in the Greek-speaking world. Everybody was a citizen of some "city," or *polis.* And when a Greek said, as did Aristotle, that "man" (human beings at large) is a *zoon politikon* (one who lives in a city), he was really saying that to be human *is* to be a social creature.

Aristotle saw clearly that nobody can or does live entirely by himself or herself, nor does anybody live only within the confines of family or a group of more immediate friends. Each of us is part of a larger and more inclusive group—an Athenian, a Spartan, a Theban. The Greeks of that period could not think of "individuality" in the narrow sense so often given the word today. For them, the individual was always envisaged in the communal context that made him or her a citizen with inescapable social belonging. Each was understood as being this or that person—to use the later idiom that we would prefer—who employed his or her talents and gifts, whatever they might be, to work with others, to share with them in a common enterprise, and to realize his or her potentiality in that manner, even if each one also had a specific family and a home and an affectionate relationship, perhaps of an intimate sort, with a "lover"— who for the Greek was usually somebody of the same gender.

So much by way of explanation. This emphasis on the wider societal aspect of human existence has often been minimized in recent thinking. During the past several hundred years, and most clearly in the culture that we inherit, we have been indoctrinated with the idea of "individual substances," and in consequence we have neglected our wider social belonging. In his fascinating book *The Meeting of East and West,* published many years ago, Prof. F.S. Northrop of Yale University showed how the influence of John Locke's philosophy, with its stress on the notion of *individual substance,* has had seriously damaging consequences for our Western ways of understanding ourselves and the world. To talk of *substance* is to suggest (however different may have been the meaning of that word in the classical and medieval period) something that exists in and for and of itself alone, without any necessary dependence upon that which is not itself; while to put the adjective *individual* before *substance* is to talk as if this substance could be seen primarily as a particular instance of a more general class. When St. Thomas Aquinas in the thirteenth century adopted the view, which he got from older classical thought, that each of us is "an individual substance of a rational nature," he also gave the impression that each of us is one of a class who can exist without belonging— although Thomas was wise enough not to let matters stand like that, for he went on to speak of the dependence of *human* substances upon the divine substance and, what is more, much preferred to speak of us as persons, with the implication that we share together since we are open to others as they are to us.

Thus, the difficulty has been that in much philosophical thought, with its influence upon other ways of thinking and also upon our ways of acting as humans, there has been a failure to grasp adequately the peril of talk about individuals and equally about substance. Hence, it has taken many years for us to come to understand that, as I said in an earlier chapter, we are in reality a routing of experiences, possessed of some degree of awareness and of self-awareness and marked by a capacity to enter feelingly into the lives of others. Not only *may* we do this; it is so integral to our very existence as human, and indeed as creatures in a cosmos like ours, that we *must* do this. Furthermore, the stress on our rationality and on morality, found in Aquinas but much more exaggeratedly stated in Lockeian thought, has overlooked the deeper feeling-tones (or what Northrop called "the aesthetic component") in the world and in our existence as part of that world. The result has been a very artificial and inadequate understanding of what we are, how we act, and the part we play in the creation. We belong, as I have urged again and again; and in our belonging we enter into relationships with others that have about them a "felt-ness" that is much more profound than whatever rationality we may happen to possess. Northorp was concerned to emphasize a more wholistic picture. He pointed out that in the East there has been a keen awareness of the appreciative, evaluational, and even emotional side of experience. If only East and West could have a genuine "meeting," he believed, more would be made in the West of this side of things while the East might come to appreciate that there is also something to be said for rationality and its human functioning.

Doubtless, Northorp was a bit too optimistic in his picture of this meeting and its results. Yet because of greater knowledge by each of us about the world at large, there now is a recognition that we have been the victims of an unfortunate bifurcation and a sense that we are all in need of a much more inclusive grasp of what it really means to be human. Further, there is a more adequate realization of how important is the aesthetic side, as well as growing awareness that what I have called our "sociality" is an inescapable and invaluable part of human existence. All this tells us much about how in the city, or larger human community, we are to express our humanity and find ourselves thereby enriched in our grasp of true selfhood-in-community.

I have already pointed out how we humans are organic to the natural order, emerging from it and belonging to it. It is a dynamic, processive, developing order, in which we share. Hence, older ways of thinking about human existence are in need of a very thorough reconception. We now speak in terms of the becoming and belonging to which I have made such frequent reference, and we also see that our relationship to nature, not to mention our responsibility in it and for it, needs to be given fuller recognition than hitherto has been the case.

Perhaps what has just been said will assist us in coming to a better understanding of the wider social relationships to which the present chapter is devoted. Any healthy development of humankind requires that we see ourselves as existing with others. So we go on to say something about cooperation by each of us with our fellows and also notice the contrasts among men and women, each with distinctive qualities that must be appreciated and valued.

We have our identity in a world where by necessity we live in the city—in neighborhoods, towns, cities, countries, continents, and, ultimately, in the entire "global village." Many years ago the American statesman Wendell Willkie wrote about "the one world" we all inhabit. He was right in taking this point as of enormous significance for men and women in the future, as it has always been (albeit not consciously appreciated) in the past. Our social situation is simply *given.* There is nothing we can do by way of extricating ourselves from it. And our right course is to grasp the fact, live in terms of it, and seek to implement to the fullest degree this general belonging that is ours. But it is the combination of community and contrast that is most interesting, since often this is not adequately understood and, therefore, needs a particularly emphatic statement, even today when we are obliged to agree with Willkie and acknowledge that what happens anywhere in the world of human affairs has its affect upon what happens to us, whoever and wherever we may happen to live. Community or cooperation need to be seen for what they are, essential to our healthy existence; on the other hand, contrast of cultures and types, which bring freshness and variety, needs also to be seen for what it is, as the way in which human life is delivered from monotonous sameness and dull repetition of pattern. Taken together, these two—community and contrast—are basic to the whole enterprise.

When we think of these two we have a clue to what may go wrong, to what, in fact, has gone wrong, in much of human history—and not least in our own day. For we now are well aware of the sad truth that all is not well with us in our city, or wider social life. We may have been delivered from some kinds of tyranny, but we have not been saved from the possibilities of an ant hill existence, on the one hand, or a riot of conflicting interest—local, national, international—on the other hand. In some periods the person has been lost in the community so that the resulting situation is a sheer totalitarianism, in which each person is a depersonalized instrument or agent for some supposed "national spirit," like the *volk* about which Hitler liked to talk. In other periods, the opposite may be seen. When a former president of the United States, Herbert Hoover, spoke in favor of what he called "rugged individualism," he was really stressing the paticularities of each of us to the exclusion of the belonging, which is proper for all of us. The result of this latter stress is a highly competitive, indeed belligerent, attitude in which devotion is directed to the presumably single person who is to make his or her way in the world without regard for others. In each of these kinds of society the end product is disastrous.

There can be a communal*ism* (and I stress the last three letters of the word to show it to be a perversion of genuine community) that makes nonsense of personal and national characteristics; there can be an individual*ism* with its turning of human life into a battle for supremacy, where the less powerful are beaten down, oppressed, and denied opportunity to express their selfhood while the more powerful secure the place of advantage. There is very little to choose between these two mistaken and, indeed, radically false notions, with their result in actions that promote distortion and end up in destruction. Both are so inadequate to the real facts in the cosmos process that the only sensible attitude toward each of them is to say a vigorous no. This is not some theoretical problem, either. In the present world, with its stark divisions and strongly conflicting interests, it has become a frightening threat to the whole human enterprise.

In a healthy personal-social life, men and women find their setting for a growth toward the actualization of their potentiality. But, as I have said before, this actualization involves all of us in a common enterprise in which a basic shared good is being sought. Therefore, we need to enquire what is the goal or aim and how it may best be achieved. The ethical enters here, but much more basic to the situation is what I have styled the aesthetic—that is, social harmony in its richness and variety.

For this reason, I must now say something more about that word *aesthetic*. The usual understanding of the word relates it to some art form, but often this can degenerate into "prettiness." Further, an "aesthetic person" or (vulgarly) an "aesthete" is often taken to be what is sometimes styled "arty," a term that has become pejorative in significance. But all these ideas rest upon a misinterpretation of the proper sense of the word *aesthesis* in Greek and also in a good deal of careful contemporary study and discussion. What aesthetic really means is harmonious, beautiful, rightly patterened, attractive to sensitive observation or hearing. Indeed, I should wish to urge that it is a way of getting at what the Greeks intended when they spoke also of something or someone as *kalagathon* or *kalagathos.* In Greek, *kalos* means "beautiful" and *agathos* means "good," and when the two are brought together in a compound word the sense is precisely "harmony" or "right patterning" or even what in the best old English usage would have been styled "lovely." And the opposite of this would be in English "ugly," which points to a person or object as unattractive, unlovely, badly patterned, and, hence, offensive.

When I remark, therefore, that a rightly ordered society is marked by harmony and, hence, is an aesthetic reality, I am saying that such a society is so patterned or so functions that it is, indeed, a lovely or beautiful affair. And any society that pays little or no attention to the aesthetic in this sense is likely to become an *ugly* society in a number of different but distressing ways. For example, we are familiar enough with the ugliness of totalitarian architecture, of which the buildings put up under Hitler in Germany and Mussolini in Italy are appalling instances to any sensitive observer, however massive and imposing they may be. We are also familiar enough with the unlovely bourgeois self-assertion in architecture where all that seems to matter is obvious usefulness or functional efficiency. Both of these are manifestations of ugliness in the society that erects them; both of them have no regard for such important contexts as a neighborhood may provide and no regard for what suitability in that particular place would demand. Lewis Mumford has served us well in drawing our attention to the way in which such architecture reflects vulgarity in social life, a lack of sensitivity in human awareness, a willful assertion of cheap attitudes, and contempt for those who must be exposed to such building and have their feelings offended and their taste degraded.

Our present concern, however, is not with this obvious and distressing manifestation of disharmony in social life but with the disharmony itself—that is, the failure on the part of men and women to discern that true community and sound relationships within it can be found only as each of us has his or her place in a wider grouping of humans, where there is vivid contrast because each is valued as being precisely *this* or *that* person while the community as a whole has goals or ends (what used to be called "ideals") that are worthy, upbuilding, and enriching. The enduring goal of such a sound society is to hold community in balance with diversity. Life in that community is made interesting by striking contrast but without hateful conflict. Thus, communal*ism* is ruled out; so also is stark individual*ism*, one again italicizing the last three letters of each word to indicate that a perversion of true community and of true

73

"personeity" (which, as I have said, I prefer to the talk about "individual") is intended. Such a good society is harmonious; it is an ordering in which the aesthetic has been given proper attention by those who represent and act for the membership at large.

When we speak of a "culture" we are pointing to a pattern of harmony or disharmony that marks a given period or historical sequence in the life of the wider group. A culture is the ordering of the society's ways according to patterns that are generally accepted by those who belong to it, even if these are not always vividly in the forefront of their consciousness. It has to do with such agreed purposes and such accepted goals, with such agreed values as are taken to be important and even essential. So soon as there is widespread dissatisfaction with or disregard of these purposes or goals, expressed either in actual revolt or in an inchoate sense that they are inadequate or false, the culture begins to break up. This has happened again and again in history; often it has been called "the collapse of a civilization." Of course, to use the last word suggests a relationship, if not an identity, between "culture" and "civilization." Often enough this seems to have been the fact, although scholars usually prefer to make a distinction between them, using the former (culture) to describe an almost unconscious, yet very real, series of assumptions about life and its meaning and the latter (civilization) to indicate a specific arrangement of life in outward and visible ways. For our present concern, however, we need not worry about this distinction, valid as it may be.

What we are pleased to call Western civilization—and most of the time those who use the phrase intend the culture with which we are familiar, with its ideas and "ideals" of "the good life in community"—seems now to be in an advanced state of disintegration. We live willy-nilly "among the ruins," as somebody has put it. Many are in outright revolt, especially thoughtful and sensitive younger people; many are terrified by what we are experiencing; some acquiesce in what they would call "the loss of all standards"; many are trying to fight against these things and return to (or, as they would probably prefer to say, maintain) the

74

earlier state of affairs. Of course, some think that this situation is not new in history. They assume that this is just the way things have always gone and how they must always go: for them, disintegration is the normal state of affairs.

All these attitudes seem to me to be mistaken, to the point of being highly dangerous to human integrity and to the communal expression of it. But there can be little doubt about the confusion and bewilderment that millions of thoughtful men and women feel today. The consequence is their inability to see that the truth of the matter is that Western civilization, about which we talk glibly and in defence of which we assume that we have fought a major war and have taken part in minor conflicts as well, no longer really exists.

W.B. Yeats wrote in a famous poem about how "the center" no longer "holds," about how "the good" lack "passionate intensity" while evil men and women have just such zeal, and how in the result things are "breaking up" wherever one looks. Vast numbers of people today, sometimes with a vivid feeling but more often with a vague sense of unhappiness, feel that as a society we in the West are drifting heaven-knows-where. They do not know what to do about this. They cannot readily adapt themselves to a social pattern that is in such a condition of disintegration. Nor do they know how they can usefully make a contribution that would effect the emergence of a new pattern or culture, in which our inherited past will not be dismissed or discarded as now entirely meaningless. Neither can they return, even if that were possible, to that same past if it is taken to be the only conceivable way of ordering social life. Here is disharmony with a vengeance, as so many today seem to experience it. They cannot join with those vociferous persons, often associated with conservative religious groups, who seek to go back to what are often styled "the good old days"; on the other hand, they do not have much sympathy for the wildly radical people who assume that there must be a total destruction of our inheritance, in the naive confidence that surely "something" will then appear that is entirely good and sound and right. Both of these seem highly unrealistic. Also, for what it is worth, their tactics and their activities are often blatantly offensive to countless numbers of men and women who are caught between the two movements.

I believe that harmony is the goal any society worth preserving must manifest, and I am also convinced that such harmony, with its aesthetic appeal, is the result of holding in proper balance the two factors of genuine community and genuine contrast. But we must recognize two possible kinds of social harmony. The French philosopher Henri Bergson called these two the *closed society* and the *open society*. We must now say something about these two.

The closed society is one in which novelty is not welcomed, and, hence, an attempt is made to preserve unaltered the modes of thought and behavior that have come to us from the past. Any change in these, any alteration of perspective and in ways of looking at human existence and its difficulties, is regarded as treason to that past and a guarantee of loss of significant meaning. This closed society is the kind of harmony for which reactionaries yearn. It is the explanation of talk about "the good old days," the nostalgic "look back," and the yearning for obedience to all the accepted and hitherto conventional ideas and practices that are to be so completely respected that nobody is ever threatened by novelty. In such a society, life would be without risk. In recent years, as I have said, this approach to things is represented especially by what some call the New Right or the Moral Majority. But for many of us, this kind of closed society and the sort of "harmony" that it provides are lacking in any genuine possibility of creative advance. It can be deadly in its impact and sometimes seems to be nothing more or less than the condition of death itself. It is like a carefully preserved corpse, and whatever vitality it may seem to possess resembles the galvanic movement of a corpse before complete rigidity sets in. Those who take this position have forgotten, if they have ever known, that all existence, including human personal and social existence, is a becoming. Hence, they are doing what Whitehead once described as "fighting the grain of the universe."

There is another sort of social harmony, however; it is what Bergson called the open society. Here there is a genuine welcome of novelty, an awareness of the challenges presented by our different circumstances and conditions, and a willing readiness to experiment. At the same time there can be a deep respect for the past; indeed, the inheritance that is ours is to be honored and esteemed, not as a straitjacket but as providing the firm ground for further development. That inheritance does not demand that new possibilities be rejected; rather, it gives us a position from which further development, exploration, and change may be welcomed. In other words, it is not reactionary in attempting to live in the past, nor revolutionary in setting out to destroy the past, but realistic in recognizing the causal efficacy of that past and then going on to new possibilities. It might even be called "radical," if by this we intend what the word itself indicates: that is, a getting at the *roots* of our tradition and then a seeking to discover ways in which these may be adapted to and used in a new age with its own particular questions and its own novel opportunities.

My contention is that when the city is healthy, it will find itself in the second category, as an open society. It will be dynamic and not static. This is not likely to make human existence in society an entirely easy and uncomplicated affair; on the contrary, it will give rise to continued struggle. It will require a spirit of adventure and an element of risk; it will demand bold planning and courageous action. Its dominant quality will be zest. And we may recall here how Whitehead, in his discussion of civilization in *Adventures of Ideas,* insisted that any civilization that lacks such zest— vitality, vividness, even some awareness of "chanciness"— is likely to be moribund, if not already dead. In fact, the open society is going with "the grain of the universe" in implementing the reality of becoming and belonging, taken in their genuine unity.

Here we have the challenge of our time. Are we to seek, and work earnestly for, a reactionary return to former ways? Or are we to seek, and give ourselves zealously to, a possible future that will be different from that past yet the beneficiary of what it has to give? Are we to spend our days regretting the loss of old patterns with which we have long been familiar? Or are we to be bold in our quest for new patterns that, despite their unfamiliarity to many of us, may yet enable life to be lived with zest by men and women of this and the coming age? To put it in another way, are we to rest content with the goods that we believe have been already achieved, when even now they seem to have become a little stale, or are we to strive in the novel circumstances that are ours today for other and perhaps more inclusive goods? Are we ready to see that more and more people in more and more places in our global village are looking for just that opportunity and have no wish to remain comfortably (although that seems really impossible nowadays) in what the stolid majority seems to take for granted?

Something like this is the basic issue thoughtful men and women confront today. It is the choice between a fearful rejection of the new with a pathetic clinging to the familiar and a brave consideration of new openings, certainly with the grateful use of many of our inherited guidelines but with no desire simply to conform and no pattern simply to be imposed upon everybody with or without consent and whoever or wherever he or she may be. Doubtless none of us, of ourselves alone, can be very effective in establishing this second sort of harmony and the society that can embody it. None the less, the contribution of each person has its considerable importance. Above all, each of us can have a part (however small) in whatever concerted effort is required for the establishment of a dynamic type of harmonious social existence. This is a good to which each of us may lend support.

A social pattern like this will offer a common life in which each member has his or her place and to which each can make some real contribution. The concern will be for the best and fullest development toward self-realization within the commonweal. It will resemble a healthy organism, where each part has its appointed share in the social enterprise, "the building up of itself in love." That is a Pauline expression for the Church, to be sure, but it can have a broader application as well.

Already much has been done along these lines. I happen to live in Britain where the welfare state, despite its obvious failings and inadequacies (to which reactionaries are always calling attention), has had and still does have as its chief concern the provision to everyone of those absolute necessities that are required if the citizens are to lead better, healthier, and more satisfying lives because they have been delivered from nagging fears and worries about illness and old age and much else that can be so dreadfully threatening to them. Again, in the field of education in many countries there is a renewed recognition that mere accumulation of facts is not sufficient to give young people a good life; they need to be helped to grow in appreciation, to delight in sharing, and to learn to love what is truly beautiful and enriching. They need to know about the past that is their inheritance but also about the challenges of the present and the possibilities in the future. Still another example is the field of social medicine, where more is done than simply care for those already ill. Here the intention is to further whatever will prevent illness in the first place and seek to promote health of mind and spirit as much as health of body. In all these it is recognized more and more that in our human existence we are really becoming and belonging creatures, and in some quarters there is even a recognition that religious faith has a large part to play in achieving these aims.

Harmony is the goal, and as I have urged, that is an aesthetic concept. What can be said about the ethical dimension whose importance must also have recognition? Often enough this has been taken to mean obedience to imposed moral rules, given as it were from "on high." But in the perspective that we have taken in this book, the ethical dimension is a matter of the human realization of possibility and accountability, with men and women in their social belonging and in the light of the one absolute ethical principle—which is nothing other than love-in-action. If that is true, then there can be no sentimentality nor easy tolerance, on the one hand, nor inhibiting conformity to accepted conventional norms, on the other. For love is a giving-and-receiving, a mutuality, a willingness to seek for the true good of others, and that may entail hardness, firmness, and genuine demand. In other words, what will be found most valuable is "the permissive society."

I am aware that for many this is a horrifying idea. But we should grasp the obvious truth that in a society where what is supposed to be good and right is imposed either by some supposed divine *fiat* or by required conformity to "what the Joneses do," there is, in fact, no possibility of genuine moral principles involving both human freedom and human accountability. Instead, we look at others as only automata or robots. Morality cannot really be legislated, although, of course, there must be regulations that prevent dangerous abuses of the common good. Morality certainly is not simply "doing what present-day society approves"; that is only a kind of coercion in which the person is regarded as an object with no real freedom of choice. The principle of love-in-act can never be forced upon people; it must be evoked from them and made attractive to them. About this I have already said enough in our previous discussion. Here I would only add that the ethical dimension, at its best, is grounded in a conviction about how the cosmos "runs" in its deepest reaches—which is to say that sound morality and sound religious faith are intimately related. In simple words, human love-in-act, human concern for justice, human relief of oppression, and sound human ways of relationship are all properly to be taken as creaturely reflections of and creaturely agencies for the divine Love that is God, the primal cause and the final affect.

We should ask ourselves whether or not the city in which we now live or the city that we hope to build—whether this is in our immediate neighborhood, our town or village, the nation, or the whole world of humankind—can measure up to the criteria that I have argued are basic. What changes are needed, what specific programs are indicated, what tasks are demanded, what sacrifices are required, if *this* is what the city is all about? Here there are no ready-made answers; in any event, struggle will be demanded and often pain will be experienced if and when we strive to act resolutely and responsibly in these matters.

A society that safeguards both community and contrast needs some vision that will serve as a lure, that will be a goad to action, and that will offer a goal that is worth achieving. Here the religious dimension of human existence is of primary importance. "Where there is no vision, the people perish": so runs an Old Testament text. The religious vision at its best tells us what God is "up to" in the world, disclosed in various intuitions or insight into the divine activity. At the heart of this religious interpretation of existence, cosmic and human, are some things that cannot be denied. Self-centeredness, arrogance, possessiveness, desire and action to control or coerce, hatred, jealously, injustice, oppression, claims to utter self-sufficiency, and neglect of others and their needs are bound to lead to destruction. It has been said that "the mills of God grind slowly, but they grind exceeding small." This is the adamant quality of the divine working; it is why it is indeed "a terrible thing to fall into the hands of the *loving* God"—and notice that I have changed the biblical phrase from "living God" to "loving God," although both are equally true.

Once we come to some such religious vision, however, those who share in a profound faith such as the great religions make possible (and in our own part of the world, that means the Christian faith) can have a deep confidence that from the ruination of existence, which is the result of those evils just mentioned, the cosmic Love can extract genuine and abiding good. *All is not lost,* no matter how bad the times may be. There is always room for hope, even in the darkest days, because God can, and God does, "make all things new."

7

The Religious Community

The Christian Church is a religious fellowship with particular beliefs, practices, and moral teaching, and like every other identifiable routing of events in the cosmos it may very well be called "a social process." To get at this we may recall for a moment the way in which identity is established for any routing of events, making it *this* rather than *that*. To speak of these will help us when we come to consider the structures that are the Church's characteristic "marks," as they have been called, with the manner in which they express the purpose of the fellowship and the nature and work of the people who serve in leadership, as well as the mass of members who are known as the laity.

The remembered past, the decisive present, and the intended future: these we have seen to be the three factors that determine the identity of any routing in the cosmos. In the specific instance of human personality, as we all know, I am who I am, first because of the past that has been causally efficacious in bringing me to the present moment. In this I remember—consciously or unconsciously or in what I styled earlier a "visceral" manner—what has gone to make me. Again, in the immediacy of the present, I am who I am because I decide among the various possibilities that are open to me, always, of course, in the light of the past and its consequences. The choices I make are for or against the goal or end that might be attained through the right use of the materials given from the past and known in the present. Through the decisions that I make and the actions that implement those decisions, I am who I am, either moving or not moving forward to achieve in the future the goal or end proper to me. Throughout this process, there is an identity of self through remembrance, decision, and anticipation—in the correct sense of that last word, which means a glimpse or a preliminary intimation of what in the future may come to be.

When we apply this paradigm to the social process that is the Church, we can readily see how apt it is. The religious community has its remembered past, its activity in the present, and its aim for the future. Thus, it is preserved from being merely of archaeological interest, if the past alone is stressed; from "reeking of the contemporary" and its associations, if the present alone is given attention; and from some unreal idealistic quality with little concrete reality, if the future alone receives attention. Something must now be said by way of developing this point.

The remembered past of the Christian fellowship includes the initiating aim that came with it into existence. Its history goes back to the remote period of Jewish tribal life when a small group of nomadic people believed that in some fashion they had been "chosen" (as they put it) to represent and to give witness to their tribal God Jahweh (or Jehovah, as we incorrectly phrase the name). Jahweh, which had been the name of the god of a relatively small and insignificant association of Semites, eventually would be said to be "the God of the whole earth." But that would take time. The Jewish people believed that they were uniquely the people of this deity. Their mission was not so much to seek to promote their own welfare or aggrandizement but to testify to all the world that their deity was supreme in power, in righteousness, and (as they came later to believe) in "loving-mercy." The Old Testament material tells the history of this people, their wanderings in the Fertile Crescent, their eventual sojourn in Egypt, their escape from captivity in Egypt (which they regarded as their deliverance by Jahweh), their entrance into Palestine, and the subsequent events in their national life in the "Holy Land."

The total biblical narrative, when New Testament is joined to Old Testament, goes on to speak about the appearance of Jesus of Nazareth, accepted by some Jews as their promised Messiah or "anointed ruler." This Messiah, now identified by these Jews and those whom they converted as that One in whom God's prevenient loving activity was both proclaimed in word and enacted in deed, was preached elsewhere in the Greco-Roman world of the time and accepted there by many as also their lord and savior. So the "new Israel" was not founded by Jesus, as if by the teacher of a new religion, but was "refounded" *on him*—"The Church's one foundation is Jesus Christ our Lord," says the familiar hymn. His teaching, his acts, his influence are all witnessed to in what is our earliest New Testament material; thereby it is possible to arrive at an understanding of the originative event for the specifically Christian community and to see how that event, when responded to in faith, established a society that carried on its own work, proclaimed its own faith, and engaged in its own worship. The end result was a conception of God as what I have styled in this book "Love-in-act" or "active Lover," whose purpose in the creation, so far as humans are in the picture, was to establish that kind of love as the principle of human existence, with the justice that necessarily accompanied it and through the power that enabled it to become effectual.

As I have said, the Old and New Testaments give us this story. They are, thus, an indispensable element in the Church's memory and have their essential part and place in establishing the Church's identity. Yet the past is not the whole story, since it is remembered in the present moment. It is not a "dead past"; it has become a "living past" through that causal efficacy or memory that I have indicated. The Church exists in the present, and there it must make its way, exert its influence, relate its message to the immediacies of each succeeding age and in this fashion decide how, where, and when it is to act—and for what ends. Unless it engages in this task, it not only becomes irrelevant; it also loses its proper identity. It may even degenerate into being nothing more than a respectable cover for the ordinary decencies (and sometimes indecencies!) of the secular society in which it exists, serving as a sanction for all-too-human tendencies to assert and delight in personal or social self-sufficiency.

But it can also—and this is its true vocation—bless the common graces of ordinary human existence, while at the same time it speaks prophetically about the distortions and defects of that existence, recalling men and women to their true humanity and their true destiny and, hence, to their true fulfillment as "lovers in the making" who share life together in mutual acceptance and service and who thereby experience a foretaste of God's sovereign rule as Love and in love.

This brings us to the future aim as an indication of identity. The Church's future has to do with the ultimate goal that is God's kingdom or sovereign rule, when and where and as the human creation is brought to exist under, and to serve, the cosmic Love that is God. No amount of human endeavor, in and of itself, will establish or "bring in" that kingdom. It is from God and of God; it comes as a gift and not as a reward for what we have done. Nonetheless, the responsibility of the Church, in respect to that future, is to do what a Prayer Book collect calls "prepare and make ready the way" toward it "by turning the hearts of the disobedient to the wisdom of the just." By its persistence in directing men and women toward that end, the Church is identified as the specific human society that in a specially vivid fashion discloses, and by its devoted action works toward, the reign of holy and just Love.

Here then are the three factors that provide the Christian fellowship with its specific identity. It is the organism, understood as what I have styled a social process, through which "the love of God in Christ Jesus" works in the world. This is not the only and exclusive sphere of such working. The disclosure of divine Love and the release of that Love in the originative event has found many ways of expression wherever there has been awareness of what it is about; it would be entirely mistaken to regard the Christian community as if it had some sort of controlling possession of that expression of Love. There have been other channels in the world of human affairs where divine Love has been and still is operative, since God is not bound by the ecclesiastical and institutional channels we know. In the world religions, certainly, as well as in what sometimes might be taken to be entirely secular and often nonreligious working in the creation, the same God is at work. A Christian can only say that in the fellowship called by Christ's name there is a vivid and even a decisive manifestation of this ceaseless loving activity in the world, disclosing what God is "up to" everywhere and always.

Thus, the Christian Church, with all its imperfections (about which we shall speak later in this chapter), is nevertheless a living, dynamic, relational community whose existence is in the world and whose work is for that world and concerned with that world; by that very token it is an agency of universal Love in that world. Hence, the Church is in a way the "complement" and the "completion" of the values by which any and every routing of occasions will function when it is the way of serving God and, hence, of securing the best development of humankind in its becoming and belonging and in its movement toward fulfillment or realization of God-given possibilities. It is also by necessity in conflict with some of the values so often taken to be important but that, in fact, are deleterious to just such human existence. Those values, if they merit that description at all, are the *sinful* or wrong ways in which humans seek their goals. Thus, there is a double nature of the Church: *in* the world yet not *of* the world. And that is to be reflected in the lives and labors of its general membership and of its ordained ministers.

The Church does not exist nor carry on its work in order to receive approval from the rest of human society. It is not interested primarily in securing its own position, privileges, or power. If it centers in these things, it has forgotten its identity, its integrity, and its essential purpose. In fact, the Church is the only social group whose main objective has nothing to do with its own maintenance; it does not exist "for itself" but for its mission. That mission is to proclaim its message with the hope that this may be accepted by men and women in all places and at all times, so that those people may attain to the best and most fulfilling life under God. In the New Testament phrase, it is there to bring the "abundant life"—in Hebrew this is *shalom*—that is made available through response to the loving activity of

God—again in Hebrew, the divine *chesed* or the "loving-mercy" of God.

In doing this work the Church may be said to have three clear objectives. These are (1) the healing needed by broken humanity; (2) hence, the making of men and women aware of God who alone can thus heal, with the establishment of deeply intentional relationships between God and God's human children; and (3) the promotion of a shared and mutually enriching life among men and women. We shall say something about each of these.

In the first place, the healing that the Christian fellowship is to bring is the overcoming of what I have styled the "brokenness" of human life. That brokenness is found in what Tillich pointed to when he wrote so forcibly about the estrangement and alienation of men and women from their true destiny and genuine fulfillment. The religious term for this is *sin*, describing the state or situation in which we humans find ourselves, thanks to our inheritance of the consequences of past wrongdoing, and indicating also the particular ways in which we ourselves continue in such wrongdoing. In less religious idiom, this has to do with the lovelessness, false self-centeredness, and coercive behavior of humans as they try to live for and to themselves. When some of the New Testament writers speak dismissively about "the world," they mean just this state of affairs. Humans strive to live as if they were "masters of all they survey." In so living, they are bound to act in particular ways (*sins*, in the plural) that manifestly express such false self-sufficiency. For those who are in this condition, which includes all men and women everywhere, the Church seeks to bring the healing that comes from God—the "grace" that is both the divine favor toward us and also the empowering that makes newness of life, in and under love, a reality among us.

In doing this work the Church acts—here is the second specific function—to make it possible for human existence to be lived in an awareness of God and in a response to God in faith, worship, and obedience. Much depends here upon the way in which God is pictured. About that we have already spoken. When God is portrayed as a remote first cause or as a tyrannical dictator or as a moral legislator or as a sentimental and undemanding deity, great harm can be done. In such instances, human existence can come to reflect exactly such falsity. Humans can live as if God did not count at all save as the remote creator; they can live as if they were cringing subjects of a dictator who had no value in and of themselves as becoming and belonging creatures; they can live in terms of a legalistic morality imposed upon them, as it were, from "outside" or from "above" with no regard for their freedom or dignity; they can live as if God did not much care what they did, how they treated others, or whether they sought the better rather than the worse ways of fulfillment.

The Church's responsibility is so to communicate an awareness of God as "the Love that will not let us go" that it becomes a judgment on whatever prevents or interferes with a right relationship in mutuality among men and women. Here is the basis for both a personal and a social gospel, for the immediate application of the love of God for and to each person and also for the wider implications of that Love in terms of justice in society at large, where through our belonging we have our existence.

Finally, as the third function of the Church, there is bringing of "new life" to men and women, not so much in words spoken as by concrete expressions of sharing when they are brought together to live in amity and mutuality, with the giving-and-receiving that is both expressive for and the impulse toward greater caring. This is what is meant when we speak about "life in God through Christ." It is not a matter of human effort so much as a patient and glad human receptivity, but one that is not simple or effortless. When the "new life" is lived out, it may very well entail suffering; most certainly it will demand sacrifice. But it opens the way to new possibilities for sharing with others under God. Here it is worth observing that the Church does not set up artificial barriers to its membership. This openness is signified in baptism by the fact that an infant, too tiny to be conscious of what is happening, is granted membership in the confidence that the wholeness and healthiness of the community's life provides opportunity to grow to maturity—there can be "growth in grace."

What has just been said will give some idea of what the religious community is meant to be and to do. Alas, there is much that seems to militate against this. Those who belong are not "already made perfect"; furthermore, there can be among its membership and in the ordained ministers much that is "off-putting." They may not seem very satisfactory representatives of the Church's mission and message. The language often used in Church circles can also be "off-putting"; it may have an archaic sound and may seem out of touch with what is known to be true about the world and its affairs. Again, much in the community can seem trivial and self-regarding, rather than serious and generous. All this presents a problem that must be faced realistically by those who speak and act for the Church. This must be understood and remedied, so far as may be done. People have to be met where and as they are. The Church's job is to communicate with men and women in their actual condition, yet without denying its own nature and belief. Those outside need to be helped to grasp what is intended underneath what to them may often seem difficult language and behavior.

Today, when many (and not least, younger men and women) are aware of the frustrations of life and lack any convictions that can give them some sense of value, there is a remarkable opportunity. For the Church itself, this requires that it seek to bring the message in a generous and understandable way to the outsider; for the outsider, there may be a dim sense that somehow the Church provides a chance to find significance in life and to make possible acceptance of convictions into which one may enter more deeply as the years go by. A truly liberal-minded man or woman should then be ready to "give the Church a break," as young people put it nowadays—that is, to let it have a chance to show what it can bring to them in promoting and enabling "newness of life" and growth toward the human fulfillment they desperately want to have. Such people, once they belong, may be of great assistance in the essential task of *aggiornamento,* as Pope John XXIII put it, by which the Church may be updated without its losing or denying its central mission and message.

In carrying out its appointed task, the Church proclaims

the gospel it has received, it celebrates the sacraments (and chief among these, the Eucharist), and it provides leadership (but not dictation) in the discipleship that expresses outwardly what it is for. To perform these tasks, the Church requires those who will act for it, and those who are called to that role are the ordained ministers. That function in the Church does not exist apart from, but as essentially a part of, the community. In other words, the minister or priest is a representative agent of what in truth the Church itself is doing. No longer can we talk about ministry as if it were separate from the larger membership; we can not speak of ministerial status but rather must stress ministerial *functioning*. This last point introduces a big topic we need not discuss here. Perhaps I may refer a reader who is interested in this subject to what I have written recently in another book, *The Pilgrim Church and the Easter People* (Wilmington, Delaware: Michael Glazier, 1987), which contains my Tuohy lectures given a few years ago at John Carroll University in the United States.

Over the past few decades a good deal has been done to establish new patterns of ministering by ordained people, male and female. Nor has this been confined to any particular denominations among those that make up the Christian fellowship throughout the world. The fact that those lectures of mine, by an Anglican, were delivered by invitation in a Roman Catholic university may illustrate my point here: the conception of ministry as functional is increasingly seen to be the right one, while the older idea of a sharp separation between laity and ordained persons is less and less accepted, even in traditional bodies like the Roman Catholic church— and in this case, despite a contemporary movement, of which (alas!) the present pope sometimes seems to be a spokesman, to continue things in the older fashion.

The final topic for discussion in this chapter has to do with the non-Christian religious traditions and the non-religious movements in which any faithful person must of necessity see that God as divine Love-in-act has also been working in the world. Wherever there is concern for goodness or love, justice and righteousness, deliverance from oppression, devotion to truth, appreciation of beauty, and other positive ways for the enhancement and enrichment of our human becoming and belonging, we must be prepared to recognize that God is active. Much of the time it will be in what I have earlier styled a secular fashion. But as I have urged, this is perhaps a mistaken phrase since in one sense there are *no* strictly and entirely secular areas from which God is really absent. God seems to prefer, often enough, to work through just such interests and agencies.

When we turn to the non-Christian religious traditions, only those who are narrow-minded and arrogant in their position would dare to deny that God has been at work there. The Christian claim is, rather, that to those of us who have been given the privilege of standing within the Christian fellowship, there is in Christ what I have called a particularly vivid and decisive disclosure of what the divine Love is always and everywhere doing for the sons and daughters of the human race, no matter where they may live and no matter what may have been the historical factors that have produced the sort of religious convictions that are theirs. To some people, any such openness will seem scandalous; they need to learn, however, that "the love of God is broader than the measure of man's mind," and that it is possible to stand firmly and faithfully for what has been given to *us* without at the same time seeking to deny to God generosity of spirit.

The whole point of our argument in this book has been that in becoming and belonging we have a key to understanding not only ourselves and our world, but also in some degree to understanding something of God and God's activity in the creation and in the event we name when we say "Jesus Christ."